MAMMALS OF THE NORTHERN ROCKIES

MAMMALS OF THE NORTHERN ROCKIES

Tom J. Ulrich

MOUNTAIN PRESS PUBLISHING COMPANY
MISSOULA, 1990

Fifth Printing, June 2007

Library of Congress Cataloging-in-Publication Data

Ulrich, Tom J.
    Mammals of the northern Rockies

    Includes index.
    1. Mammals — Rocky Mountains — Identification.
I. Title.
QL719.R63U57   1986   599.0978   86-8759
ISBN 0-87842-200-5 (pbk.)

Printed in Hong Kong by Mantec Production Company

Mountain Press Publishing Company
P.O. Box 2399 • Missoula, MT 59806
406-728-1900

Dedicated to my father, Henry Ulrich

Table of Contents

Acknowledgments

The countless hours I have spent peering through the backend of a camera focused on wildlife, provided the majority of the photos used in this book. What remaining species I was not able to record were thankfully supplied by associate photographers. The credit for their work is given individually.

I also owe a deep thanks to three special friends—Don Davidson, Dave Erickson, and Bob Love — for making available their time to proofread my manuscript, eliminating rough edges and correcting punctuation.

To the Glacier National History Association and Clyde Lockwood I also owe a special appreciation as they were instrumental in the publication of this book.

Introduction

The information in this field guide is arranged differently than others I have read or thumbed through in the past two decades for two main reasons. First, this book is geared toward being a visual record, so oftentimes I used two, six, ten, or eleven photos to supplement my printed information. Hopefully some of these photos will clarify a wildlife experience which may have posed a question for you in the past. Also, unlike most field guides which follow a set order of progression from the most primitive species to the most advanced, I took the liberty of reversing this order. My intention was to make photographs of the larger mammals more readily available since they are encountered most often.

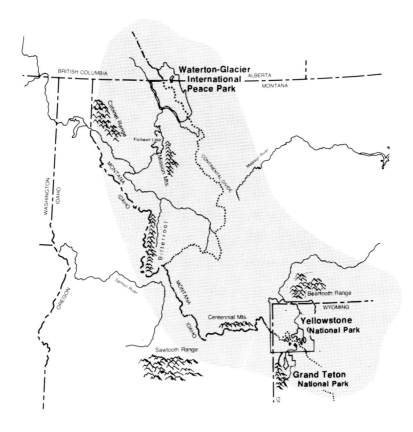

Northern Rockies

Centrally located between the Colorado and Canadian Rockies, the total area of the Northern Rockies exceeds 100,000 square miles. Its valley floors average 3000 feet in elevation with many of the higher peaks exceeding 11,000 feet. The variety of mammalian fauna is as diverse as the vegetative zones which carpet all elevations. Higher elevations which pose a beneficial habitat are such protected areas as Glacier-Waterton International Peace Park and Yellowstone National Park. There are no fewer than a dozen wilderness areas such as the Bob Marshall, Great Bear, Selway-Bitterroot, and Cabinet, preserving thousands of acres for excellent mammal habitat.

Color Variations

Our visual conception of wildlife is largely influenced by the colors we see: red fox, grey squirrel, black bear, etc. Nature usually keeps these colors constant for any one species, but occasionally something out of the ordinary happens.

An excellent example is *Sciurus niger* or fox squirrel. The usual rustic orange color distinguishes it from any other squirrel, but many people are confused by the fact that *niger* means black. When the species was named by Linnaeus, a 19th century naturalist, the first fox squirrel he saw was the color of coal and thus the name *niger*.

This little quirk came about from a single genetic shift called a mutation. Each cell in an individual's body contains all the genetic information for that organism. Somewhere in this code is the knowledge to manufacture a protein pigment called melanin. Melanin gives tone to skin and hair. Overproduction of this pigment will conceal all other colors, resulting in the black or melanistic animal. A total absence of melanin and other pigments causes the organism to be white, or albinistic.

Melanism and albinism occur at about the same rate; however, white albinistic animals have a much higher mortality rate because they are easier to see and thus subject to predators. When in the field, watch for these variations. You will be witnessing a rare exception to the laws of nature.

Albinistic gray squirrel   T. Ulrich

Normal gray squirrel   T. Ulrich

Melanistic gray squirrel   T. Ulrich

The Rut

Fall is an exciting time for big game enthusiasts. The docile lifestyle of our larger male mammals ends abruptly due to hormonal changes and a renewed interest in the opposite sex. Animals once tolerant of their fellow males become much more aggressive. Cold weather forces them to winter ranges where they become arch rivals. Major interest is now focused on gathering a group of females called a harem. The size of the harem will vary depending upon the species. Elk tend to be the most polygamous, gathering a harem of twenty to sixty cows. Bull moose, on the other hand, gather only a few cows.

A dominant female usually governs the harem. Since the whole group is guided by her movements, the dominant male concentrates on keeping the harem together and driving away subordinate males. Strength and horn or antler size will determine whether he retains ownership of the harem or relinquishes it to a male vying for his position.

When the dominant male is challenged by a male of equal size, the fight may be as simple as a poke from a horn, or it can be a drawn-out battle of butting heads and meshing antlers. The winner will claim the right to service the harem, and the process ensures that the strongest genes will be passed on.

The strength and endurance of the dominant male is taxed continually while keeping the harem together. He waits patiently for a female to come into heat. At that time the dominant male removes her from the group to be serviced. During his absence, secondary males will scatter the harem. Not much will happen if no other females are in heat, but if a female is ready to mate while the dominant male is away, chances are good that a subordinate male will breed with the female.

After servicing a female, the alpha male returns to gather the scattered harem and wait for another female to come into heat. Repeated until the last cow is bred, the process takes a dramatic toll on the male since he eats little and expends tremendous amounts of energy.

When the breeding season closes, the dominant male feeds extensively to build depleted body stores before winter sets in. It has been a very demanding period, but now the male can rest and return to the life of a bachelor tolerating his male companions once again.

14

Mulie polishing his points

Moose in head-to-head combat

Isolating a ewe in heat

Horns or Antlers

I have spent a considerable amount of time in our national parks, and it always amuses me to hear a visitor say, "Look at the size of the horns on that elk!" It could be a slip of the tongue, but many people don't know the difference between horns and antlers. The two types of big game headwear differ in structure and development.

The deer family is distinguished from all other groups by the presence of antlers on males. There are a few exceptions — female caribou sport antlers, and occasionally a doe will have small spikes — but neither compare to a mature male deer.

Growth of the antler usually starts in spring. Elevated knobs on the head, called pedicels, swell from an influx of blood and nutrients. An outside membrane of blood vessels, called velvet, secretes calcium to the inside, establishing deposits of the hard boney material. If you were to touch the velvet it would feel warm due to the increased blood flow. The velvet is also very delicate. Any injury would cause bleeding and result in a deformed antler. In order to avoid injury, males are relatively docile while their antlers are growing.

Once growth is complete, blood stops flowing to the velvet causing this membrane to dry and peel away, exposing the antler. Males often rub their antlers in some brush to help remove the velvet, and a good thrashing about also strengthens neck muscles and polishes tine points. The antlers are now prime for rutting season. They will be shed sometime during winter.

Horns are made of keratin, the same substance that makes up fingernails and hair, and develop from a boney core. Instead of being shed each winter, horns grow continuously throughout an animal's life. At death, the living tissue between the core and horn decomposes and the horn falls away.

Now that you know the difference between horns and antlers, you can chuckle at the misnomer the next time you pass through Elkhorn, Wisconsin. (A real place, honest!)

Loosened horn showing the bony core T. Ulrich

Shedding the velvet T. Ulrich

Caribou antler in velvet T. Ulrich

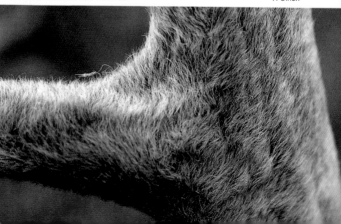

Fur

One of the more prominent characteristics of mammals is the presence of hair. For some mammals, like whales or walruses, the amount of hair may be limited to merely coarse bristles near the mouth. When hair is dense and covers much of a mammal's body, it is given another name: fur. Fur is a rather broad term, covering many different types of hair. Hair gives color and contour to an animal, but more important is its value as protection.

The most obvious and most clearly visible type of hair is the coarse guard hair. These are long, pigmented, durable hairs meant to take abrasion and weathering. When an animal, such as a raccoon, is chased by a predator, it cannot waste time picking its way carefully through cover. It brushes by, bounces off of, and scrapes against rocks, wood, and other obstacles in the way. Yet one seldom sees animals with scratches, cuts, or abrasions. Wrap your fist in a piece of fur and rub your knuckles against a cinder block; the fur will protect your knuckles the same way it protects an animal's body.

If you were to spread the guard hairs, you would reveal a soft, woolly underfur. These fine hairs have one purpose: to retain heat. Much of the underfur is shed each spring and replaced by a thinner, cooler coat in summer. In the fall, the fine hairs grow dense again for winter. Since guard hairs do not change much during the year, an animal's healthy appearance in the winter is due to the full growth of underfur.

Another type of hair is found on antelope and on most members of the deer family. They have little or no underfur; the only hair present is rather thick and hollow. You will often see elk or deer with a substantial layer of frost on their back in winter, but don't worry. The insulation factor of the thick, hollow hairs is so great that the animal is not affected by the frost.

Coarse guard hairs of a coyote T. Ulrich

Soft woolly underfur of a coyote T. Ulrich

Guard hairs of a deer T. Ulrich

Tracks

It has been said that when man goes into the wilderness, the only thing he should leave behind is his footprints. Wildlife inhabitants seldom leave more than their footprints, but examining the prints they leave on the earth gives wildlife enthusiasts much satisfaction. Tracks tell specifically who passed this way, generally how long ago, and vaguely what they were doing. Interestingly, looking at tracks can also tell us something about the long evolutionary development of the foot. It can help us understand why some animals are faster than others.

A large group of mammals take their steps by placing the heel first, planting the whole foot, then stepping away on the ball of the foot. This is a slow, time-consuming process not conducive to speed. The porcupine, raccoon, badger, and skunk all travel by this method. They are called "plantigrade."

Through evolution some mammals have picked their heel off the ground. You can simulate the process by placing your hand palm down on a flat surface. This is the plantigrade position. Keep your fingers on the surface and slowly raise your palm, bending at the joint of the fingers. Notice the thumb or fifth digit also leaves the surface. This is the "digitigrade" position. Animals save a considerable amount of time by walking on their digits. The fox, bobcat, and wolf are digitigrade. Examine the front leg of your pet dog or cat to see the remnant thumb or "dewclaw" on the inside of each leg. This is typical of digitigrade mammals.

Returning to your hand with the palm raised, bring the fingers up so just the tips remain touching. This is the "ungulate" position. The fifth digit has completely disappeared on animals in this group. The first and fourth digits rise to become dewclaws while the last two develop enlarged nails or hooves. Deer, elk, and antelope walk on their nails. Ungulates are built for speed.

Looking at wildlife footprints should help you to better understand why a fox can run faster than a raccoon, but not as fast as a deer.

Plantigrade
Digitigrade

Unguligrade

21

Mountain Goat *Oreamnos americanus*

No other mammal lives at higher altitudes than the mountain goat. This white cliff-hanger is at home among the sheer precipices, arêtes, and glacial cirques of the Northern Rockies.

Lewis and Clark, finding goat hides among coastal Indian tribes, considered it a form of bighorn sheep. Because of its rapier-sharp obsidian-black horns, muscular shoulders, white beard, and shaggy coat, the scientific classification of this animal was a subject of much debate. The name *Oreamnos,* meaning mountain lamb, was given to the goat by Rafinesque, an early 19th century naturalist. Today, the name still holds, but taxonomists group it with distant Old World antelopes such as the goral, serow, and chamois. It is believed that early ancestors of the mountain goat ventured across the Bering Land Bridge between Asia and North America about 600,000 years ago. Finding safety in rugged mountain terrain, the goat prospered and evolved into its present form.

The morphology of the goat reveals exceptional adaptations to its mountain domain. Muscular forequarters enable the goat to pull his stocky body up rocky outcroppings and fearlessly traverse perpendicular slopes. The goat's artiodactyl (two-toed) hooves provide traction. They are unlike the hooves of any other member of this group. The bottom of each toenail is convex and composed of spongy material, a superb modification for gripping ice or any smooth rock surface. The spongy material, combined with the goat's ability to spread the hooves apart for increased surface area, contributes to the sure-footedness of this creature.

The goat's winter pelage is especially suited to cope with the harsh climate of its environment. The coarse guard hairs are seven to eight inches long and hollow, providing superb insulation. They

Billy winter fur   T. Ulrich

Nanny winter fur   T. Ulrich

Billy summer fur   T. Ulrich 8-13-2013 **Yearling**   T. Ulrich

also enhance the goat's muscular form. Beneath the guard hairs lies a three-inch layer of soft, woolly underfur which acts as a second thermal barrier by trapping a blanket of air next to the body. The innermost part of this undercoat is visible in summer after the guard hairs and some of the soft wool have been shed.

When scanning the vast openness of the Northern Rockies, the goat can spot a small moving object a mile away. Except for an occasional golden eagle trying to capture a kid, all predators roam far below the realm of the goat. Perhaps as an evolutionary response to this, the goat's eyes actually point downward. If a person wanted to stalk a goat, he should approach from above since this bearded climber has to turn his head to look up.

Since both sexes have beards and horns, distinguishing male from female can be troublesome. However, determination can be made upon close inspection of the horn, since the billy (male) has a much thicker horn at the base than does the nanny (female). The billy also has a large, crescent-shaped gland behind each horn. The gland becomes more prominent during the rut and breeding season. By rubbing vegetation with this gland and depositing a secretion, he will establish his territory.

The rut and beginning of breeding season is late November and continues through much of December. At this time the males, for the first time during the year, start to associate with females. A dominant male does not assemble a huge harem (as do many other species). He gathers a few select females to protect from other subordinate males.

Six months later, near the end of May, a nanny will venture to an isolated rock outcrop and deliver a seven to eight pound kid. About one in every forty births will produce twins; triplets are rare. Nourished with rich milk, the new offspring grows quickly and can follow its mother anywhere within a week.

After returning to the main herd, the kid will associate with others its own age. Playing a game called "bump," they drive their heads into the hindquarters of their partner, going around in circles. This helps build muscles and coordination, but more important, it establishes a social order among them which will be maintained throughout life.

Horn growth the first year can be as much as three to four inches, a considerable amount compared to the greatly reduced rate of growth in subsequent years. During winter, foraging is difficult and horn growth is non-existent. The result is a narrow ring on the horn, making it possible to determine the age of any goat.

Horn gland   T. Ulrich

One in forty twins   T. Ulrich

Traction pads   T. Ulrich

Kid   T. Ulrich

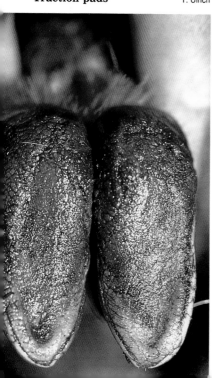

25

In the Northern Rockies, Glacier National Park offers the best opportunity to observe mountain goats. Both the Hidden Lake Trail and Highline Trail on Logan Pass lead to excellent goat habitat. In the spring, *Oreamnos* can be seen at the Walton Goat Lick on the southern boundary of Glacier Park. Here, this grandfather of the peaks is lured from the high country to the Middle Fork of the Flathead River where mineral salts provide a welcome supplement to his meager winter diet.

Birth on isolated cliff   T. Ulrich

Playing bump   T. Ulrich

Spring molt   T. Ulrich

Rocky Mountain Sheep

Ovis canadensis

Nature is filled with exciting episodes of animal behavior, but if you had to pick the spine chiller, it would have to be the annual ritual of bighorn rams butting heads. To understand the beauty of this event, one must know about all the steps leading up to this moment.

Early November brings snow and cold to the higher elevations, and bighorn start their annual migration to lower elevations and traditional breeding grounds. As bands of males come together, there is a mixing of social hierarchies causing all kinds of problems. Depending on strength and horn size, these rams battle to establish their rank.

Most encounters are between rams equal in size. A preliminary stage involves pushing and shoving, with occasional leg kicks to the gut by the challenger. Just as the altercation seems most intense, the two gladiators will separate and graze quietly, but each ram is watching the other very carefully.

When one ram feels it has an advantage, it will rise on its hind legs and lunge toward its foe. The other reacts correspondingly. At the last moment, heads rotate slightly and horns collide with a crack that is often heard a mile away. Chips from the horns fly and blood may ooze from the ram's ear or nose, but again and again each puts his 250 pound body behind the impact until one is exhausted or hurt and behaves in a subordinate manner.

To keep from pulverizing their brains, years of evolution and adaptation have created a double cranium. The inch of spongy material between the two skulls takes the shock to protect nerve tissue.

Ram

Ewe and lamb

Kick challenge

The victor thus earns the right to service the ewes. With the social order established, rams will band together again, but only the dominant ram services the harem.

As females come into estrus, an estrogen is given off. A prominent "lip curl" is exhibited by the male as he lifts his nose to the wind and sniffs for this hormone. When a receptive ewe is located, she is driven onto some shear cliffs for mating. This prevents other rams from interfering. With mating complete, the alpha (dominant) ram ventures back to reclaim his harem.

By the end of May the pregnant female will leave the herd and find an isolated cliff face. Birth is generally to a single lamb which she licks thoroughly to clean and dry the fuzzy, dark-gray coat. It takes a few hours for the lamb to stand well enough to nurse, but by the end of a week it can rejoin the herd to associate with others its age.

Since the animal is usually identified by the impressive horns of the ram, a closer look will reveal some interesting information. This is a true horn growing from a bony core. Composed of keratin, the horn is similar to human hair or fingernails. The horn grows continuously, but when food acquisition is greatly reduced in winter, horn development slows and results in a narrow ring. It is easy to age the animal by counting the growth rings.

As horn growth continues, the tips will eventually interfere with vision. At that time bighorn have been known to grind their horn tips against a rock face, shattering the ends, but giving the ram better sight. This is called "brooming" and is an important characteristic of older rams.

Most sheep do not live to a ripe old age. Teeth are grinding vegetation continuously—grasses in summer and browse in winter —constantly wearing down until feeding is impaired. Being very social, sheep are also subject to a high incidence of disease and parasites. A form of lungworm is common, and when weakened by it the sheep become susceptible to pneumonia.

If an infectious disease occurs at a critical time the results can be very damaging. One such incident took place several years ago in Yellowstone. It was rutting time and because of the close contact, a blinding pink eye infection was spread. Many big rams subsequently fell to their deaths from cliffs.

Bighorn lip curl

Bighorns butting heads

Bighorn submission pose

There are several good locations to observe bighorn sheep thoughout the Northern Rockies. Glacier National Park consistently has a group along the Highline Trail near Haystack Butte. Others can be found near the Many Glacier Hotel. Yellowstone Park offers excellent viewing on the sheep flats near Gardiner. The National Bison Range also has some transplanted sheep. No matter where you experience them, you will be left with a lasting memory.

Broomed horns　　　T. Ulrich

Growth rings　　　T. Ulrich

Double skull　　　T. Ulrich

Six month lamb　　　T. Ulrich

33

Bison

Bison bison

The best time to view bison would have been 150 years ago. Moving across the great plains of the central United States to the eastern slopes of the Rockies, you would have encountered huge herds, perhaps as many as sixty million of these roaming animals. Indiscriminate slaughtering quickly brought an end to this natural phenomenon.

The only large numbers of free-roaming bison today live in Yellowstone National Park in Wyoming and in Wood Buffalo Provinceal Park in Canada. Here, natural processes regulate their existence and one can catch a glimpse of what once was. Despite such stresses as weather conditions, predation, and disease, these herds have established stable populations through natural selection, making them the most important bison herds in existence today.

There are several more government regulated areas where buffalo still roam, one of which is the National Bison Range near Missoula, Montana. Unlike the free-roaming herds mentioned above, National Bison Range herds are actively managed. Herds are continually rotated on pastures to prevent overgrazing. Excess animals are harvested to keep the population constant. Management policies can include innoculating for disease control or sustenance feeding during severe winter conditions.

More closely related to domestic cattle than to any wild big-game animal, a mature bull can weigh 2,000 pounds. The very large head and muscular forequarters, both covered with long hair, contrast sharply with their tapering flanks which are covered with shorter hair. The sexes are dimorphic, although both are dark brown in color and both have horns.

Buffalo are very gregarious. This would have provided increased protection in times when millions of them covered the plains. A

Bison bull

Bison cow

Wallowing

small group of ten to twelve members, composed of cows, calves, and young bulls, is considered a basic unit. As these units band together, larger herds are formed. The units express a separation of sexes — except during the mating season — but very often mature males are found on the periphery of these groups.

The rut and mating season begins in August primarily to allow for a long 9.5 month gestation period which follows. Two mature bulls will put their heads together and start shoving. This behavior is mainly to reinforce dominance, but then both will generally service the females.

Born singly, the light brown, forty pound calves start appearing in May. The expectant mother moves off and gives birth to her calf some distance from the main herd. Within a few days the little calf can walk, enabling it and the mother to rejoin the herd. Initially appearing similar to domestic calves, the young bison will change to the darker adult color at about three months of age.

Use extreme caution when viewing unfenced populations of bison. A huge bull almost appears to be in pain as he walks slowly from place to place, but bison are deceptively fast and agile — not to mention strong. The number of persons gored by buffalo in Yellowstone Park each year is alarming. Do not let their gentle appearance fool you into moving too close for a photo; get too close and it could be your last.

These wild cattle have yielded totally to spatial demands of human occupation. The vast herds of plains bison (and the buffalo nickel, too) disappeared long ago and will never be seen again. Hopefully, our awareness and concern will continue to protect the small numbers that remain.

Young calf   T. Ulrich

Older calf   T. Ulrich

8/11/2013

Young bull   T. Ulrich

Cow portrait   T. Ulrich

Pronghorn   *Antilocapra americana*

There is no other animal in the world related to *Antilocapra americana*. It is in a class by itself because of a unique hair horn which is shed after the mating season. Our first explorers recorded them as "antelope" and although not a kin to one, the name is still accepted. Because of the prominent point on their horns, a more accurate common name for this animal is "pronghorn."

For millions of years the home of the pronghorn has been the vast open plains. To survive in this environment the animal has perfected two very important characteristics: very keen eyesight and incredible speed. The pronghorn is one of the fastest animals in the world.

With eyes equal to eight power binoculars, *Antilocapra* can notice small moving objects four miles away. Its eyes also protrude from the skull allowing peripheral vision backward, as well as forward. This exceptional eyesight, paired with a natural curiosity, occasionally subjects the pronghorn to danger. Hunters sometimes are successful at luring pronghorn close by waving a red cloth attached to a pole. The pronghorn's curiosity may draw it to the bright object.

Visual awareness is not enough to save its life, but great speed will usually get it out of trouble. One personal experience occurred while driving a lonely stretch of Wyoming road. Cruising at 55 miles per hour in my car, I approached a herd of pronghorn divided by the highway. All started running parallel to the pavement and soon the pronghorn on one side decided to cross over and join the others. It was impressive to see half a dozen animals running twenty feet in front of my car, but more amazing was their ability to easily pull away with a sudden burst of speed.

Designed for speed, the pronghorn's legs are narrow and lean.

Pronghorn buck   T. Ulrich

Pronghorn doe   T. Ulrich

Buck and harem   T. Ulrich

Pronghorn leg bone is actually stronger than that of a cow (though only one fourth as large), enabling the leg to take the tremendous pressures of running at high speeds. Most animals would break a leg if they stepped into a hole running, but the pronghorn's leg is strong enough to avoid the damage.

Through all their previous evolution, these speedsters were without restraint and could run or migrate endlessly. Present day fencing has taken its toll because pronghorn have never developed the ability to jump high. A three foot fence might as well be twenty feet for *Antilocapra*, and many are severely hurt or killed as they attempt to run through these barriers.

Antilocapra is unlike many groups of animals in that the males and females remain together all year. During a September rut the alpha buck will drive away subordinate males and form a harem that can include fifteen does. Breeding is accomplished during this time.

After a gestation period of eight months, the expectant female will venture away from the herd. If it is her first birth there will be one fawn, otherwise twins are the rule, and occasionally triplets are born. Each progeny will be given birth at separate locations, and for the first few critical days they will be raised independently. This greatly decreases the chance of losing both newborn to predators. Lacking spots, the young are called "fawns" and after a week will join the main herd.

Wyoming is recognized as having the greatest population of pronghorn; Montana is a distant second. Two prime territories with fairly constant populations are Yellowstone National Park (Lamar Valley and the flats near Gardiner) and the National Bison Range near Moiese, Montana. Pronghorn can also be found north of Townsend, Montana, on Route 287 near the Twin Silos. With development of residences, fencing, and farming, this area is an excellent example of how *Antilocapra* has adapted to modern range conditions.

Pronghorn with weeds   T. Ulrich

Pronghorn fawn   T. Ulrich

Built for speed   T. Ulrich

Woodland
Mountain Caribou   *Rangifer tarandus*

In the lower forty-eight states, the woodland mountain caribou is the rarest mammal. Not recognizing international boundaries, a small remnant herd roams from British Columbia to the Selkirk Mountain Range of Northern Idaho. A last remaining stretch of old growth spruce/fir forest is home for twenty-eight of these mysterious and majestic animals.

Caribou are members of the deer family. They are somewhat smaller than elk and larger than deer. A unique characteristic is that the females sport antlers. Her elegant headdress is not as massive as a mature bull's, but is significant and noticeable. Their enlarged feet are also worth mentioning. The bottom area of each foot is some six inches across and is excellent for walking on snow or in boggy areas.

Arboreal lichens constitute a large portion of a caribou's diet in winter, but this does not limit their population. Habitat destruction due to forest fires and timber harvest, several highways crossing their migration route, and misidentification by hunters take the biggest toll.

If you wish to see these magnificent animals of the woods, you must spend considerable time in the Selkirk Mountains of Northern Idaho. The twenty or so caribou migrating over millions of wilderness acres makes your chance of seeing one slim at best.

Bull with two cows   T. Ulrich

Cow caribou   T. Ulrich

Caribou track   T. Ulrich

Shiras Moose   *Alces alces*

The largest member of the deer family is the moose. North America is blessed with four species, each inhabiting a distinct geographical niche. The largest is the Alaskan or Yukon moose which occasionally reaches 7.5 feet at the shoulder and can weigh 1800 pounds. The northwestern moose is found from the Boundary Waters of Minnesota west across Canada to the Pacific Coast. Eastern moose inhabit the northeastern part of the continent, while the Shiras (or Wyoming) moose is found from the Northern Rockies south to Colorado. (The Shiras moose is named after George Shiras III, a naturalist and late trustee of the National Geographic Society.)

Most observers think of the moose as being a highly aquatic mammal. This is partly true since much of what they eat, especially in summer, is aquatic vegetation. They show no fear of feeding in water over their head. What most people do not realize is that a good amount of their time is spent in heavily wooded areas. Here they find seclusion and relief from insects and heat. Do not be surprised if you encounter a large bull moose in woods far from water.

Being semi-aquatic, this creature has developed some unique characteristics for handling this medium. To keep from sinking deep into the mud of swamps, bogs, or marshy areas, their dewclaws are greatly enlarged compared to most members of the deer family. As the moose puts its hooves down, the dewclaws of each foot spread and easily support its heavy weight in any soft substrate.

Another helpful adaptation is that their hind legs are positioned so that when a step is taken, each leg is actually raised straight up making it much easier to step out of sucking mud. When observed on open ground, this gives them a gait that looks awkward, almost to the point of being comical.

It has been stated that the moose is the largest member of the deer family, but when viewed, it is usually feeding in water and

44

Bull moose   T. Ulrich

Cow moose   T. Ulrich

8-14-2013

Cow feeding   B. McDonald

therefore partially obscured. A healthy bull moose will sport a chassis seven feet at the shoulder, and draped over this is 1200 pounds of muscle and organs. Their color will vary from black to shades of brown with white "stockings" on their legs. A conspicuous, pendulous "bell" hanging from the throat area of both males and females has recently been categorized as a secondary sexual characteristic.

What has to be the one most outstanding visual aspect is the huge, palmate antlers of a bull. Growth of these massive structures begins in April as males go into reclusion, oftentimes in the company of other males. This gentlemen friendship is soon broken near the end of August as velvet is shed and the rut begins. With the use of scent marking, a dominant male will establish a territory and any intruding males are dealt with in head to head combat. Occasionally, their pushing and shoving becomes so fierce that antlers will lock permanently and result in death for both animals. Once superiority is established, the bull will take several mates, but he tends to only one at a time.

After a gestation period of eight months, birth in the spring is usually to twin calves. They have no spots and are a light brown in color. It is not until three months later that their fur enriches to the darker adult coloration.

In Yellowstone Park, such locations as Willow Park, Pelican Creek, and Hayden Valley are excellent habitat for moose. Along Going-to-the-Sun-Road in Glacier Park is "Moose Country" which provides the best opportunity to see moose in that part of the country. One should exercise extreme care while viewing these large mammals because females with calves and bulls in rut can be very dangerous.

Cow with calf   8-14-2013   T. Ulrich

Calf   T. Ulrich

Bull in velvet   T. Ulrich

White-tailed Deer   *Odocoileus virginianus*

If one had to choose the most elegant resident of the forest, it would have to be the white-tailed deer. Always alert, the animal moves about passively as each step is taken, each rise of its head, or turn of an ear has a beauty all its own. It is truly a sight to behold when a deer takes off in great soaring leaps with its tail upright, flashing like a waving white banner.

A deer only runs until its predator is out of sight, then the deer waits attentively to see if it is being pursued. The sharpest sense for the white-tail is its smell; it can usually detect the unfamiliar, upwind, long before it is seen. Hearing is also keen and generally tells the eyes where to look. Although their world is viewed in shades of gray, the slightest movement is noticed. A windy, blustery day will understandably create nervousness among the deer as air currents whirl, causing vegetation to snap and branches to crash together.

The white-tail is common in the Northern Rockies and usually prefers to inhabit the lower elevations. The sexes live separately through most of the year. Males start to develop antlers in early spring. At this time the pedicels on top begin to swell, initiating growth. For more mature bucks the antlers increase in size rapidly and by September growth is complete. Velvet is shed by twisting and turning the antlers in some brush. This strengthens neck muscles and polishes the points enabling the buck to take on any rival.

Harems of a few does are formed near the end of October. At this time the doe comes into estrus. If she is not bred the first time, thirty days later she will again reach estrus.

June is the time for birth, and if it is the doe's first, there will be only one fawn; thereafter she will always have twins. The newborn

White-tailed buck   T. Ulrich

Wasted death   T. Ulrich

Portrait   T. Ulrich

White-tailed doe 8-13-2013 T. Ulrich

49

fawns are equipped with soft white protective caps over the tips of their hooves. These caps are to protect the mother through gestation and birth; they dislodge after the first few steps. Immediately after birth the fawn is licked dry and is almost odorless. Within twenty minutes a fawn can walk well enough to be led away from the area where birth fluid saturated the ground. The next three to four days are spent sitting motionless in cover. Several times a day mother will return to nurse the young, exercise their legs, and give comfort.

Very soon after the first nursing, a green pasty anal plug is eliminated. Once, while driving a lonely road in eastern Oregon, I came across a doe that had just been hit in the hindquarters by a car. She was killed instantly by the impact, but a fawn was dislodged and thrown onto the highway. I walked to the little one, who was shaking from a cool morning breeze, and I was immediately implanted as its mother since I was the first living creature it saw.

I gave it the original name "Bambi" and proceeded to nurse it with a concentrated solution of powdered milk. We had many exercise periods along the road, and I distinctly remember the sticky green evacuant. It startled me because everything I observed being ingested was white and liquid.

My relationship with Bambi was short-lived because I was required by law to leave it at a veterinary clinic. The doctor verified that the anal plug was normal, and in a follow-up visit several months later, I found that the fawn had grown to be a beautiful doe.

If you wish to view white-tail deer, you should know that they are most active a few hours at dawn and again at sunset when they venture out to the edge of meadows to feed. Their preference for heavy woods keeps them separate from mule deer. In Glacier Park they can often be observed near campgrounds or lodges. The heavy human traffic discourages natural predators, but the deer lose any fear of people. It is illegal to feed deer, and they oftentimes eat handouts for the salty coating. They receive little nourishment from junk food, and it usually accumulates undigested in the stomach.

Bambi less than one hour old T. Ulrich

White-tailed fawn three days old T. Ulrich

Twin fawns T. Ulrich

Mule Deer   *Odocoileus hemionus*

Western hunters call them "mulies" because of their huge, black-fringed ears. The best characteristics for positive identification are a narrow, white tail tipped in black and the dichotomous-branched antlers on the bucks. Also distinguishing these species is the mule deer's method of bounding away by pushing off with all four feet at once and landing the same way. It is this stiff-legged, spring-driven bounce that has also given them the name "jumping deer."

It has been recorded that a deer can jump an eight foot fence and perform a running long jump of twenty-five feet. To understand such athletic feats, we need to look at the beauty and structure of the deer's foot.

Place your hand, palm down, on a flat surface. Now slowly raise the heel and notice that your thumb loses contact first. This digit has completely disappeared on the deer. The second and fourth digits leave next. These become dewclaws for the deer. The last two fingers develop modified nails (hooves) and are all that make contact. This results in a great deal of agility for the mule deer.

A large metatarsal gland can be observed on the inside of the hind leg just above the ankle. It is used for scent marking, and is easiest to observe on the bucks during the rutting season when the gland becomes enlarged. Squatting allows the male to squeeze both glands together and extract a secretion. Urinating down the leg will deposit this substance on the ground.

It is estimated that there are four million mule deer inhabiting an area that covers most of the western states. The Northern Rockies is well-endowed as this species has adapted easily to open forests. Travel, especially for available food sources, is no problem for the mule deer. Seasonal migrations of many miles from summer ranges in the high country to lowland winter ranges is a common practice.

Mule deer buck   T. Ulrich

Mule deer doe   T. Ulrich

Buck in velvet   T. Ulrich

Three month fawn   T. Ulrich

Snow accumulation in the higher altitudes each fall forces the deer to lower elevations where the rut and breeding season soon begins. With a gestation period somewhat shorter than the larger elk or moose, the deer's mating occurs in late October and most of November. This assures that fawns will be born in June when vegetation is sufficient for the doe's milk production and elevated temperatures lessen the chill on offspring.

A doe will come into estrus for thirty hours and is usually bred then. If she is not impregnated, she will again come into heat a month later. The first time a doe gives birth, it will be to a single fawn; all subsequent births will produce twins and occasionally triplets.

At birth the fawn is immediately licked dry by its mother. Within minutes it is coaxed to its feet and moved from the area where birth fluids have saturated the ground. Any predator has the ability to quickly find that location.

The first three days of the fawn's life are very critical to its survival. It must remain motionless and rely on protective coloration to avoid predators. If man encounters a bedded fawn, touching it will contaminate the little one with human scent enabling any predator to locate it. The doe has not forgotten about her fawn and will return every few hours to nurse and give comfort to it.

Growth for the fawn is quick and weaning begins very casually in a few weeks. Spots are present until late August when they are gradually replaced by winter hair.

Unless you are in a highly urbanized area, your chances of seeing a deer are very good. Since the mulie and white-tail have overlapping ranges, watch for both. Open, partly-wooded areas are good for mule deer, while heavily-wooded, thick brush is best for white-tail.

Leaving scent   T. Ulrich

Getting cleaned   T. Ulrich

Three day fawn   T. Ulrich

Elk   *Cervus elaphus*

"Wapiti" is a Shawnee Indian word for elk. It means "white deer." Although this appears to be a misnomer, it is a reference to their sun-bleached spring coat. The name most frequently used in North America is "elk," derived from the German word "elch" which refers to the European moose. Recently, taxonomists have reclassified the species name to correspond with its European counterpart *elaphus*. *Elaphus* is Greek and means deer.

There are four subspecies of elk on this continent. Our largest is the Roosevelt elk which inhabits the rainy Pacific Northwest while the smallest subspecies, the Tule elk, is found in west-central California. Manitoba elk originated in isolated ranges across central Canada, but the Rocky Mountain breed is the most numerous and can be found in most of the Rockies south to New Mexico.

One of the most familiar wilderness experiences is to hear the challenging bugle of a bull elk ringing through the forest. Near the end of August, just as the nights become noticeably cooler and the amount of daylight shortens, an A-a-a-ae-e-e-eeeeee-eough! E-hu, e-hu! is given. It is recognized by another bull far in the distance, and the two answer back and forth. The call summons together two powerful mature elk, bringing each closer and closer until they finally meet. Then the opponents rush at each other, meshing antlers. The fight may last for a few minutes or for several hours. The end may be fatal for one if there is a death stab or for both if antlers become interlocked, but hopefully a dominant ruler is established and takes charge of the harem. This ensures that the strongest traits will be passed on to the offspring.

Bull elk

Bull in velvet

Cow elk

Generally regarded as the most polygamous member of the deer family in the world, a bull elk in prime condition can gather a harem of twenty to sixty cows with intentions of servicing all of them. The breeding season is long and takes a toll on the bull. Unlimited energy is needed to keep subordinate bulls from stealing his cows and to prevent the cows from wandering away. Immediately after the breeding season, he resumes his isolated lifestyle, feeding extensively to build reserves before winter sets in.

Mated cows must also feed thoroughly as a developing fetus will drain body reserves throughout the winter. Birth to a single, orange-spotted calf comes in early June. Twins are born in only one out of every three hundred births. The orange spots will be kept until replaced by new winter growth in August. Weaned quickly, the offspring is soon foraging for new tender grass shoots. Summer will find all the elk feeding on grass and forbs (weeds), but as colder weather sets in, eating habits shift to more browse (twigs).

Overpopulation is very detrimental to elk, and winter taxes their endurance to the fullest. Deep snow makes grazing impossible, and eventually trees are stripped to a definite "browse line." Food becomes scarce and with movement impaired, the inevitable consequence is that many elk die of starvation. The primary cause of this grisly event was a decision to eliminate predators many years ago. In the early days of our national parks, it was a common policy to kill wolves, cougars, bears, and wolverines in order to protect ungulates. Little did we realize that we were upsetting the balance of nature. Today, the effect is still felt as predators have never made a complete comeback.

Looking again to the morphology of the elk, one should be fascinated by the antlers. A yearling bull elk will usually have single spikes. Second year growth could see four or five points on each side, but these beams tend to be rather slender. The four or five tines appear again on the three year old, but the antlers are more heavily beamed. In the fourth and subsequent years, there may be six or more points. If a bull reaches seven tines most hunters call it a "royal," and occasionally a rare eight point elk or "monarch" is taken.

At one time elk were the most numerous and widespread member of the deer family. The encroachment of settlers and the reckless slaughter of elk for hides and meat eliminated this animal from eighty percent of what was historically its range. Controlled hunting, consistent management, and limitation of predators have combined to keep the current population stable over the last twenty percent of its former range.

Bugling — T. Ulrich

Cow and calf — T. Ulrich

Bedded down — T. Ulrich

Four month calf — T. Ulrich

Yellowstone Park is by far the best location to view an elk. Cows with calves are common throughout the park. Big-antlered males generally make their presence known prior to the rut and cold weather when they come down out of the high country. Elk Park, Gibbon Meadows, and the Madison Junction are all good locations to view "elch."

Browse line

T. Ulrich

Combat

T. Ulrich

Gathering the harem

T. Ulrich

Bobcat

Felis rufus

If one were to corner this member of the cat family — a hissing, snarling, spitting bundle of claws and fangs — it would be easy to understand why some call it "wildcat." When left alone, however, the bobcat leads a secretive, nocturnal life-style and hardly lets one know of its presence.

Resembling an overgrown tomcat, the bobcat got its name from its short, four-inch tail which is always tipped in black. It was labeled *rufus* by the naturalist, Rafinesque, since the first bobcat he encountered was reddish. A bobcat's fur will vary in coloration according to geographical habitat, although those residing in the Northern Rockies tend to be reddish-brown. A large facial ruff of black and white hair adds to their ferocity when they show anger. This cat also carries one of nature's most murderous weapons: retractable claws. Protected in fur-lined sheaths, this cutlery is always needle sharp, and with a quick flick of the paw the claws easily meet their target.

Armed with keen eyesight and excellent hearing, this feline catches much of its food by stalking. On the prowl, the bobcat investigates every thicket or cover for something edible. Often-times, taking advantage of the excellent camouflage provided by its coat, a bobcat will patiently wait to drop on its unsuspecting prey from a rock face or overhanging tree limb. The bobcat prefers fresh meat, and if a large animal is killed, such as a deer, this animal is hidden as a cache and fed on continuously until decomposition sets in. The decomposing meat may seem to be a waste, but the remains are cleaned up thoroughly by scavengers.

Mating takes place in late February and March. The male is polygamous and after consorting with a female long enough to breed, he is off to find another mate. A gestation period of sixty days results in a litter of two to three kittens wearing spotted coats. The kittens' eyes are sealed shut. The eyelids open revealing bright blue eyes after about ten days, but they will eventually turn adult yellow. At two months the mother gives small, live rodents to the kittens so the kittens can learn to kill and to become dependent on meat. The family group disperses in the fall as each ventures off to find its own territories and start a solitary existence.

In the past, the bobcat has been listed as a villainous predator who took a heavy toll on upland game birds. Recent research, however, has indicated that most of their prey is small, varmint rodents, and attitudes are now changing to accept bobcats as beneficial. Protected except during hunting and trapping season, these wild cats are often killed at other times during the year by poison bait indiscriminately set out for coyotes.

Portrait

Bobcat

T. ULRICH

Bobcat kitten

T. ULRICH

Canadian Lynx

Felis lynx

Equipped with large snowshoe feet, a lynx tries to ambush a hare which sports the same footwear. Matching every turn, twist, and leap, each animal scrambles over the deep snow with the same goal — survival. The hares are such an important food source that their ten-year high and low population cycle also affects their predator, the lynx.

Since the lynx does not have the large feet in summer, a better identifying characteristic is the two-inch tuft of hair extending from the top of each ear. This will readily distinguish the lynx from its close cousin, the bobcat. Both cats have a beautiful facial ruff and a short four-inch tail tipped with black.

The ranges for the lynx and bobcat overlap along a narrow strip of North America (approximately the same line as the United States/Canada border). The lynx is found north of this line, while the bobcat's range extends south. Both have such closely related life-styles (as far as hunting technique and food choices go) that competition between the two would be too great if they shared the same range.

With most of its range so far north, the lynx is active under the darkness of winter when daylight is minimal. During the summer solstice, however, it moves about in daylight because of the short periods of darkness.

On the prowl

T. Ulrich

Lynx

T. Ulrich

Portrait

T. Ulrich

65

Mountain Lion

Felis concolor

Related to a domestic cat because of its long tail the mountain lion goes by many common names, thus verifying the importance of having one scientific title. In different areas of the country it is called puma, cougar, panther, or catamount, to list a few of its names.

The chances of encountering this magnificent cat in the wild are slim. Generally, these felines do everything possible to avoid contact with man, a trait which may not be deliberate as much as instinctive. Many nature-loving individuals who spend their lives in lion territory have never seen one. Mountain lions can prowl silently through any type of cover, and their tawny coat blends into their surroundings.

The largest percentage of a puma's diet is deer. By stalking in a crouched position it takes advantage of all concealing vegetation and tries to move within thirty feet of its prey. The attempted strike is fast and unexpected, for there are no second chances. A successful attack is over in seconds, as the cat locks its teeth into the top of the neck, severing the spinal cord.

After a kill, the mountain lion will first eat the softer visceral organs, as they decompose faster. The rest of the carcass is dragged to a secluded spot and covered with brush and dirt where it will be eaten later.

Although the cougar can breed at any time of the year, late winter is prime. The male is polygamous and will mate with any receptive female. Although the wilderness areas are populated with these cats, their secretive lifestyle greatly limits your chances of seeing one. If you do cross paths, consider yourself in a minority.

On the prowl   T. Ulrich

Mountain lion   T. Ulrich

Portrait   T. Ulrich

River Otter   *Lutra canadensis*

The rollicking comical antics of the river otter suggest that it enjoys life to its fullest. Any snow is enough to bring out the child in an otter. It will bobsled on its belly and splash through a hole in the ice, only to get out and do it again and again. Commonly traveling in pairs, they always have time to frolic, their limber bodies rolling and tumbling intertwined through snow or mud.

Highly adapted for a cold watery environment, the otter has short legs with four fully-webbed feet, a short thick tapered tail, small ears, and a long rounded head. River otter fur is highly prized by the fur industry because of its short, thick, soft texture. But more important, otter fur is rated high for its durability — only the wolverine can match this. Most individual guard hairs on fur bearers become brittle at extremely cold temperatures and will break easily. Not so with the otter or wolverine — their fur is fully pliable and durable even in severe cold.

Mating for *Lutra* occurs in summer, followed by a long delay before implantation of the egg. Birth is in spring with an average litter size of three. Although they are very social animals, there is a short eviction period for the male just after the young are born. But he will soon return to help the female raise the young. The small cubs are somewhat helpless their first six weeks, but after that they become very playful and are soon coaxed into the water.

The otter's diet consists primarily of fish, and consequently they are disliked by fishermen. However, much of what they catch are trash fish such as suckers, which makes their presence beneficial.

Since the otter is constantly on the go and has an unlimited home range, seeing them means being in the right place at the right time. The Gibbon, Madison, Lamar, and Firehole rivers of Yellowstone Park provide the best opportunities to view the playful river otter.

River otter

T. Ulrich

River otter feeding on a fish

T. Ulrich

River otter

T. Ulrich

Striped Skunk   *Mephitis mephitis*

The easily recognized black and white warning colors of the striped skunk mean "stay clear." Located at the base of the skunk's tail are two prominent musk glands. The sole purpose of these glands is for use as a defensive measure. I have heard and read several different stories on how one becomes "skunked." Here are two accounts, each of which seem possible.

Angered, the skunk with tail raised faces toward its antagonist. Hind feet are planted firmly on the ground, allowing it to squeeze the glands and deposit musk onto the tail hairs. By flicking its tail forward, the tiny droplets are dispersed like a mist.

Another possible method is the "direct shot." The musk glands, surrounded by contractile muscles, are connected by a duct to a spray nozzle. With tail raised and nozzle aimed directly at its assailant, quick contractions will send a spray some fifteen feet.

Any way it happens the result is effective and lasting. A good remedy prescribed to give some relief is to wash with weak acid solution. Tomato or lemon juice followed by a good soap scrubbing will eliminate most of the odor.

Chemically, musk falls in the category of a sulfur-containing organic compound called a mercaptan. I accidently became familiar with this compound in an upper-class organic chemistry class in college. While working on "unknowns," it was my luck to pick a tube containing this repugnant material. The whole class was mad at me for opening the tube, so I was left to analyze it by myself. After holding my breath and working through watery eyes, I determined that it was one of the methyl mercaptans.

The striped skunk is common throughout the Northern Rockies, but be aware that there is a smaller species, the spotted skunk, easily identified by white bars or a more mottled black and white appearance.

Striped skunk   T. Ulrich

Striped skunk   T. Ulrich

Albino skunk   T. Ulrich

Western Spotted Skunk   *Spilogale gracilis*

"Polecat," "civetcat," and "phobia skunk" are several common names attached to this, the smallest member of the skunk family. Only the size of a half grown kitten, this skunk got its last nickname because its bite was once suspected of causing hydrophobia. Like all mammals, this skunk is susceptible to rabies, but the incidence among spotted skunks might be higher because they lack territorialism and are often found denning together.

Winter diet for the spotted skunk consists primarily of smaller rodents, whereas their summer consumption turns to insects, fruits, and berries. This skunk is only found in areas bordering the western edge of the Northern Rockies, and it has a nocturnal lifestyle.

Spotted skunk

Spotted skunk's den

Spotted skunks at den

Badger

Taxidea taxus

A more appropriate name for the badger would be "the excavator," because, equipped with extremely long claws, the badger can easily bury itself faster than a man could dig it out with a shovel. Its claws serve a two-fold purpose: to readily dig out the burrows of ground squirrels, gophers, prairie dogs, and chipmunks, and also to make its own burrows. The home range is so vast for the badger that it is unpractical to return each night to the same den. Consequently, a new den is excavated.

The best characteristic for identifying the badger is a white stripe, "the badge," extending from its nose up over the head. The short, squat body has a dense covering of coarse guard hairs, and the badger's thick skin makes it difficult for any animal to pierce it during a fight.

Since it likes to live in open country, the badger prefers sandy prairies, and its presence is readily apparent when a potholed landscape is viewed. These holes occasionally present a dangerous situation — a horse or wild animal can break a leg in a badger hole — but the danger is offset by the amount of harmful rodents badgers consume.

Like many other members of the weasel family, a badger mates in the fall. Delayed implantation occurs, and birth is in the spring with an average litter of three being produced. Although badgers are found sporadically throughout the area, Yellowstone's Lamar Valley and the Mammoth Hot Springs area provide good habitat and an opportunity to observe this secretive animal.

Angry badger

Badger and Rattlesnake

Digging

Wolverine   *Gulo gulo*

The wolverine is the largest member of the weasel family. Its dark brown body is side-striped with lighter brown fur that joins over the rump. A characteristic "blaze" or series of white spots in the chest area help to decorate this magnificent creature.

Throughout history the wolverine has been feared and disliked. It seems to go out of its way to spread destruction and discordance. Any animals encountered are either prey or in the way. So volatile is their personality that they have been known to drive grizzly bears away from a kill. This large weasel will also break into wilderness cabins, making a shambles of the interior as it gorges itself on anything edible. Leftover food is sprayed with a foul smelling musk marking it as the wolverine's own.

Their remarkable endurance is matched by an extremely large home range. A single male wolverine will claim a one hundred square mile swath of rigorous mountain terrain and patrol it constantly. The nomadic male will tolerate no others of the same sex in his territory and only one or two females will be allowed. Contact is seldom made between wolverines except during mating season. At times, wolverines have been seen in Glacier National Park, but many of these reports have been based only on their tracks in the snow.

Wolverine   T. Ulrich

Portrait   T. Ulrich

Wolverine   T. Ulrich

Mink

Mustela vison

A woman adorned in a mink coat is a symbol of wealth and prestige, but to observe a mink in its own coat is to observe a cunning, fine-tuned carnivore. Although the average weight is a mere two pounds, this member of the weasel family has no trouble taking down a rabbit or a muskrat, the mink's favorite food.

Armed with sharp canine teeth, the mink will ambush anything alive by locking its jaws on the back of the neck. No matter how fierce the struggle, the mink hangs on until the end. It is also known to go on reckless wanton killing sprees. Whether it's a wild muskrat family or a coop full of chickens, all may be slain and only one consumed.

Known for its beautiful, soft, durable fur, the number of mink trapped each year is slowly dropping. Wild mink are generally a uniform dark brown, but they come in all shades of underfur. A fur buyer will casually drape a skin over a finger and give a soft blow to expose this hidden color. The darker the color, the better the fur is. Those with white underfur are called "cotton mink" and are worth only the life that was taken.

Today, genetic crossbreeding and mutations have created all colors at mink ranches. A whole group is quality controlled so that each has the exact identical coloration. This makes matching skins much easier when tailoring a coat.

This native furbearer is semi-aquatic and has a very strong musk gland. Its den may be a hole in a stream bank or a muskrat lodge whose owner it devoured, but because the mink moves continuously, none of the dens are used permanently.

Depending on when mating takes place, the gestation period varies from forty to eighty-five days. A delayed implantation will assure birth in the spring. Watch for a characteristic white patch under the chin — it it believed that the juvenile has white in the chest area and as it matures, this white advances to below the chin.

Mink   T. Ulrich

Mink   T. Ulrich

Swimming   T. Ulrich

Ermine

Mustela erminea

Weighing a mere two or three ounces, the ermine is an incredible bundle of energy. It is the smallest carnivore and shows no qualms about proving it. Whole families of rodents are vulnerable to indiscriminate killing. What cannot be eaten is cached or fed to young. A simple 1.5 inch knothole in the wall of a hen house is an open invitation to havoc. One possible explanation for the ermine's actions could be that when he discovers his prey won't fit through the same hole the weasel used for entrance, he abandons that victim and goes after another one. Of course, the next one doesn't fit either. A disjointed poultry owner sees it as a wanton killing spree, while the ermine only had a dilemma.

Prey several times the ermine's body weight, such as a rabbit or ground squirrel, pose no problem to the ermine. Hunting by ambush, the ermine uses his needle-sharp canine teeth to lock firmly onto the victim's neck. All the kicking or squirming possible will do nothing to break the death grip. The end comes quickly.

In the warmer months, this short-tailed weasel sports a two-tone pelage of brown on top and a white or cream color below. The terminal end of its tail is also a characteristic black and easy to identify. With the advance of the cold weather, a complete molt changes this coat to a spotless white while the tail tip remains black. While in this white coat, the ermine is often referred to as "weasel."

It is ten months from mating to birth. During most of this period, the fertilized eggs remain dormant before implantation. The young are born in spring and at first resemble string beans. Growth is fast, and soon they dart about like a pack of hounds, pausing often to stand up and look around. Anything they catch is eagerly devoured. This ermine is easily distinguished from a close cousin, the long-tailed weasel, because the ermine or short-tailed weasel does not have brown hind feet, and, of course, it has a shorter tail.

Summer pelage   T. Ulrich

Winter ermine   T. Ulrich

Eclipse pelage   T. Ulrich

Fisher

Martes pennanti

A fisher's size, personality, and attitude lies somewhere between the larger, formidable wolverine and the smaller, tenacious pine marten. So seldom is this weasel seen by humans that it is no wonder some people question their existence. Very secretive, their solitary lifestyle is only interrupted a day or two each year for a brief mating season in the spring. Constantly on the move in deep woods far from human habitation, the fisher strikes with lightning speed any unsuspecting prey. Its reflexes are so quick that the fisher is given credit as being the only animal to feed regularly on porcupine. This daring feat is accomplished when the fisher strikes a paw to the vulnerable abdomen of the porcupine where there are no quills. If the fisher is successful, it will eat well, but for this indulgence several quills are sure to have been planted. Strangely enough, it appears these quills do little harm and eventually work their way out.

As mentioned earlier, mating is in the spring. Amazingly, it happens a few weeks after the female has given birth to a litter that averages three. A long delay in the implantation of the egg during the female's gestation period allows for birth the following spring.

These mammals are not sighted very frequently. With an extremely low population, they are present in the Northern Rockies, but exist so far back in the wilderness that human contact is minimal. If one is fortunate enough to view a fisher, its large size, blackish color, and possibly white patches on the underside will identify this creature.

Fisher   T. Ulrich

Fisher   T. Ulrich

Fisher   T. Ulrich

Pine Marten   *Martes americana*

No other member of the weasel family spends as much time in the trees as a marten. When pursuing a squirrel this arboreal predator can match every twist, turn, dive, and leap of the scrambling prey. The pounce is made with lightning speed and immediately the marten's jaws are locked onto the back of the neck of its victim.

The best identifying characteristic of a marten is the orange coloring in the chest or throat area. Rich light brown fur, a bushy black-tipped tail, and cat-like ears are secondary features to watch for. Martens show a tendency to stay away from human habitation, but hikers in the backcountry often see them. The red squirrel is active during daylight and, accordingly, the marten which feeds on it is also diurnal.

Martens have a strong anal gland and deposit musk during summer breeding season to leave scent trails for mates. Once bred, implantation of the egg is delayed until midwinter, and birth takes place in late March or early April.

This predator is one of our most prized furbearers, and because of an inquisitive nature it is easy to trap. Trying to see this animal in its habitat is another story though. Sightings are entirely a matter of chance.

Pine Marten   T. Ulrich

Pine Marten   T. Ulrich

Pine Marten   T. Ulrich

Raccoon

Procyon lotor

The raccoon is not an overly proliferated species in the Northern Rockies. Invading from both the east and west, it can be found in isolated pockets of reduced numbers in larger river valleys. Why the coon has not flourished here is a matter of much speculation. The substantial winter snow depths could be a limiting factor because the raccoon does not hibernate and is active the entire year.

Listed as an omnivorous carnivore, a raccoon will attempt to devour anything edible. Generally nocturnal, this rogue is often found along water's edge feeling blindly and deftly for its favorite delicacy: crayfish.

Our prior understanding of the raccoon was that it always cleaned its food. Its name *lotor* means "washer." The raccoon has a finely developed sense of touch, and the fact that what it likes to eat is in or near water makes the activity of feeling appear to be washing.

The raccoon is not built for speed. Being plantigrade, similar to the human, each step entails placing the entire foot down from the heel to toe. When in a hurry, it lopes along as fore and hind feet on opposite sides are used in unison.

Breeding season for the raccoon is throughout February. A male will travel miles eagerly investigating all nooks and crannies to find a receptive female. Once a female is located, he moves in for a week and several copulations take place. With mating complete, the male is off to find new conquests as the female enters a deep sleep waiting for spring and eventual birthing time.

The chances of seeing a raccoon in the Northern Rockies are slim. Each year more sightings are reported, but there is no consistent pattern to their appearances.

Raccoon   T. Ulrich

Raccoon   T. Ulrich

Raccoon   T. Ulrich

Young raccoon   T. Ulrich

87

Grizzly Bear   *Ursus arctos*

It has been said that if you are charged by a bear there is only one sure way to tell if it is a black bear or a grizzly bear: climb a tree. If the bear climbs up after you, it is a black bear; if the bear remains at the base of tree and shakes you out, it is a grizzly bear. In fact, there is a point to be made here regarding claw size. The much longer claws of the grizzly prohibit an adult from climbing most trees.

There are better characteristics to be alert for other than claw size. A grizzly will weigh between 300 to 600 pounds. Watch for a very well-developed muscular hump over the shoulders of a bruin. In presettlement times, the grizzly was a free-roaming open plains carnivore. Long claws and these increased shoulder muscles enabled the animal to dig roots and bulbs or to excavate an occasional ground squirrel from its burrow. Classified as a large carnivore, the grizzly always prefers meat because of its high protein content. However, the bear counts on vegetation to provide the bulk of its diet.

There is also a distinct difference in the facial structures of the black bear and the grizzly bear. The latter has a flattened or pushed-in face between the forehead and nose. A black bear has a much more tapered skull. A "griz" snout and the resulting jaws are narrow and lined with forty-two teeth. Armed with well-developed canines used for seizing prey, the bear also possesses a definite set of flat molars which are very helpful for grinding vegetation.

The grizzly spends most of his waking hours in search of food. He can almost be classified as an eating machine. His search for something to eat is never ending, but amazingly, man is rarely included in the menu.

One must try to understand a bear attack from a grizzly's point of view. He can view man as being a competitor in his territory. Man may be eating the bear's food or bringing harm to a sow's cubs. Attacks are quick, sometimes violent, but seldom is human flesh consumed. The best prevention is to be alert, don't surprise the animal, and give it plenty of room.

Grizzly bear 8-15-2012

Cooling off

Transplanting

The annual life pattern for this bruin has an unparalleled beauty. Mating occurs in late spring and a process of delayed implantation puts birth of the cubs off until January or February. Bears enter their dens in October or November, but do not really hibernate. They enter a deep sleep and body temperature may drop slightly, but pulse and respiration remain nearly normal—thus intriguing man's interest as to how a bear can go all winter without eating.

During winter estivation, one to four very small, eight-inch cubs are born. The cubs nurse off the sleeping sow and grow quickly. They are able to accompany her when she leaves the den in April. The cubs are weaned by July or August, but the family unit remains close while the sow teaches the young to acquire food, hunt, and locate denning areas. Inseparability continues for 2.5 years as the cubs grow and eventually equal the sow in size. Occasionally, a male cub can be larger than his mother. As the sow comes into estrus, family contact is reduced, and the cubs must leave to avoid meeting adult males.

Yellowstone and Glacier national parks have stable populations of grizzly bear. The Great Bear and Bob Marshall wildernesses are also two of the last strong-holds in the lower United States for the grizzly bear. Their actions are not predictable when they are searching for something to eat. If you are fortunate enough to see a grizzly near the road from the safety of a vehicle, enjoy it. These great bears are a symbol of the wilderness and are just barely holding their own. It is a sad reflection on our civilization that in the name of "progress" we have failed to provide adequate sanctuary for these great bruins.

Sow with cubs   T. Ulrich

Black Bear
Ursus americanus

A tapered face, large rounded ears, the absence of a muscular hump over the shoulder, and short claws are distinctive identifying characteristics of the black bear. It is also imperative to be aware of all color phases for this bruin, ranging from cinnamon blond to black.

Classified as a carnivore because of its large prominent canine teeth, its feeding habits more closely resemble those of an omnivore. The fact that black bears only occasionally kill and eat small rodents causes many to question their status as predators. Insects, roots, bulbs, berries, and carrion far outweigh any live mammals the black bear might choose as part of its diet. Black bears also have a tendency to be lazy, pursuing easy avenues of food acquisition. One thoughtless decision by a park visitor to feed a roadside bear implants a deeper behavioral pattern in the bear, often leading to personal injury or inevitable extermination of that bear.

Most bears follow a regular pattern when investigating their established territory. They use valuable experience learned during the 1.5 or more years they spent as cubs in close union with their mother. All their energy is geared toward building body stores for winter. Bears do not hibernate during cold weather, but they enter a deep sleep. Their body temperature drops only a few degrees, and the bruin can awake lethargically at any time. Prior to entering the den, their diet is limited to Mountain Ash berries and some twigs which form an anal plug. This plug will be eliminated when a large volume of water is consumed after they emerge from the den in spring.

During this winter sleeping period, a pregnant sow will give birth to an average of two or three cubs weighing only eight ounces. The tiny young, covered with very fine hair, receive little comfort as they nurse and cuddle for warmth while the sow sleeps. Growth is fast for the siblings and soon they acquire their permanent color.

Black bear 8-14-2013 T. ULRICH

Brown black bear 8-13-2013 T. ULRICH

Black bear cub T. ULRICH

It is not uncommon to find black and brown cubs in the same litter. As mother awakens from estivation, the cubs, weighing five pounds by this time, venture with her out of the den to see their first daylight.

The next few years, the cubs are very secure under the protection of mother. A very important lesson at this time is one of obedience, which mother enforces with a heavy paw. There is only so much time for frolicking and playing games before it is time for serious learning. One of the first lessons the cubs learn is that they must climb a tree at any sign of danger. The mother, with unparalleled savage fury, contends with any intruder. Even a large boar is no match for her; he will be turned away. The male bruin would kill any cubs if possible, because this would put the sow back into the breeding cycle.

It is common procedure for a bear to regularly use one tree as a scratching post. Any part of his body can be rubbed against it, but it is comical to see a bruin standing on hind legs scratching his back. These "rub trees" are easy to identify by the substantial amounts of hair caught in the bark.

The roadside bears of Yellowstone Park are a thing of the past. Gift shops in the area still carry postcards depicting "bear jams." They show long lines of vintage autos congesting a park road, most waiting to feed a begging sow with cubs. Today, the bears are gone, open garbage dumps have been eliminated, and back country use by campers is regulated. These changes were made in order to make bruins wild again and hopefully renew the fear of humans in them.

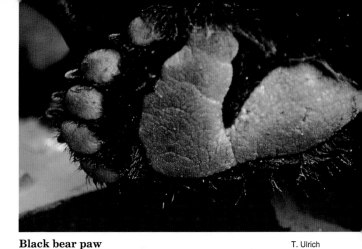

Black bear paw   T. Ulrich

Bear in den   T. Ulrich

Caching a deer kill   T. Ulrich

Red Fox

Vulpes vulpes

Black ears, black legs, and a white-tipped tail are the best identifying characteristics for the handsome red fox. Most people are not aware that this animal commonly appears with three other color variations: a stunning melanistic phase in which all the body is black; a silver fox that is black with guard hairs tipped in white; and a cross fox, similar to the red fox except for a band of darker fur running down the back and across the shoulders, roughly forming a cross. All of these variations have a white-tipped tail.

The preferred habitat for the red fox is country with many rolling hills where land use has created irregular meadows and semi-open woodlands. In this terrain it patrols for small rodents, rabbits, ground-nesting birds, insects, and fleshy fruit in season. One hunting technique it uses effectively is to stalk and rely on its keen hearing to locate a mouse in its runway. A quick four-footed pounce usually ends in an easy capture. If hunting is good, an accumulation of food is cached under dirt or snow to be eaten later.

Dens are used only for raising young. Just before giving birth, the female will renovate an old woodchuck burrow which usually has a clear view in all directions. Young are born in mid-March after a fifty-three day gestation period. Litters of six to eight are common, and the babies are called kits. The kits are very helpless at birth, and it will be eight days before their eyes open. As the female nurses and tends to the young, the male hunts to feed her. When the kits reach four weeks of age, the mother will also hunt to help satisfy the young appetites. At this time the kits will inquisitively peek out of the den opening, but it is not until eight weeks that they play outside.

If disturbed, the family may move to another den. Eventually, these underground homes are abandoned for a rendezvous site. As

Red fox kit   T. Ulrich

Three month kit   T. Ulrich

Scratching   T. Ulrich

8/11/2013

Looking out of den   T. Ulrich

the female takes one or two of the young for hunting lessons, the others rest and hang around this area. The family breaks up in the fall.

Foxes are digitigrade, allowing them to cover much ground during their hunts for food. During winter, they may cover an active home range of one hundred square miles. In most parts of the country the red fox is a valuable furbearer, but because of its scarcity in the Northern Rockies it contributes little to the industry here.

Kit hug

Squirrel for dinner

Adult red fox

Gray Wolf   *Canis lupus*

At one time this wild canid was more numerous than its close cousin the coyote. Its range was continuous across North America, but encroachment and persecution by man and elimination of larger game animals have inhibited the gray wolf's survival in most of the lower forty-eight states. Recently, some transient lobos from Canada have established a pack near the northwest corner of Glacier Park. This is a far cry from their previous history, but hopefully it signals a comeback.

It is a fact that wolves have the highest social order next to the advanced primates. They are regulated by strict laws which determine status and behavior patterns. Any wolf that fails to meet these standards is driven out of the home range. Interestingly, occasional lone wolves are observed hunting for small rodents; these wolves are probably outcasts from the pack.

A dominant (alpha) male is generally in control of the pack. The only mating during the February breeding season is between him and the dominant (alpha) female. Gestation takes sixty-three days; an average litter is six pups. The mother tends to the needs of the pups when they are young, while the remaining pack members hunt. Food is brought back to the lactating female. If she fears danger, she does not hesitate to move to another den site. As pups age, the dominant female will venture off to hunt — either alone or with the pack — while subordinate members watch over the offspring.

It can be very difficult to distinguish a large coyote from a wolf. The wolf has longer legs, shorter ears, broader snout, much heavier body, and variations in color. Close examination of the skull is necessary for positive identification.

Gray wolf T. Ulrich

Wolf pack T. Ulrich

Wolf on Moose kill T. Ulrich

Coyote

Canis latrans

Few mammals have been as severely persecuted by man as has the coyote. Nevertheless, it is holding its own by expanding its range and increasing its numbers. Along with being intelligent and prolific, the main reason for the coyote's survival is its opportunistic feeding habits. It will eat whatever the opportunity provides, including anything from elk carrion to insects. Plant food like berries and fruits is also consumed.

Presently, there appear to be two different positions concerning the coyote: there are those who wish to eradicate coyotes completely, and there are others who believe in total protection. This wild canid occasionally feeds on young cattle or deer, but its toll on the rodent population easily outweighs damage to livestock and game. For control, man has used long-range varmint rifles, traps, and poison bait. The latter, however, indiscriminately kills beneficial animals such as fox, badger, raccoon, and many others.

With a little imagination it is remarkable how much a coyote resembles a German Shepherd, thus making it easy to understand how coyotes can breed with a domestic dog. The resulting offspring are called "coy-dogs," and are generally stronger, larger, and more intelligent than either of the two parents.

The regular mating season for coyotes is February, and these animals pair for life. The gestation period is the same as that of man's "best friend": sixty-three days. Litter sizes average five to seven, but can be as numerous as nineteen. The pups are born totally helpless, and it is nine weeks before they are weaned and leave the den to learn to hunt.

One's best chance to observe this wild canid would be at Yellowstone Park. With the large numbers of big game animals, natural deaths are common, and scavenging supports a solid population of coyotes.

Coyote   T. Ulrich

Coyote on winter-kill elk   T. Ulrich

Coyote mousing   T. Ulrich

Porcupine

Erethizon dorsatum

This fascinating pincushion-on-legs is North America's only spiny inhabitant. It is actually a rodent, second in size only to the beaver. There has been some concern that porcupines can "throw their quills," but this is just a myth. However, the quills can cause a great deal of pain, but usually it is because they are anchored by a good swat of the tail.

A porcupine is covered with 30,000 modified hairs called quills. They are shed and replaced continuously from quill follicles. These spines range from ¼ inch to four inches in length. None are found on the belly, the base of the tail, or the inside of the legs.

Once embedded in an attacker, the quills begin to do their work. Small, back-slanting microscopic barbs make removal very painful, but if left alone the quills will continue to work in deeper. Death can be the final outcome if an animal receives a mouthful of quills which prevent it from feeding or if a vital organ is penetrated. These spines also start to absorb body fluids and swell, making later removal that much more difficult.

Signs of the porcupine are observed more often than is the actual animal. Springtime finds this herbivore girdling the base of trees for the sugary inner bark. During the winter it feeds on the tender branches of the upper tree canopy. Campers are sometimes surprised when they arise in the morning and discover gnawed paddles, gunstocks, boots, or ax handles. Any item touched by human perspiration can have a trace of salt left on it and serve as an attractant to a porcupine.

The mating season is in the fall. It is followed by a seven-month gestation period. Birth is to a single, fully-quilled, well-developed young one. The quills are soft but within thirty minutes they harden for full protection. After a short nursing period the offspring starts on vegetation and by autumn it's on its own.

The fact that only one offspring is produced each year indicates that the porcupine has a low mortality rate. One predator, the fisher, feeds consistently on porcupine. Using its quick speed, this large weasel can flip a porcupine to its back exposing a vulnerable stomach. A few quills are usually embedded as the fisher gets his paws in for the kill, but the quills seem to have little effect on the efficient predator.

Adult porcupine   T. Ulrich

Porcupine damage   T. Ulrich

Newborn porcupine   T. Ulrich

Norway Rat
Rattus norvegicus

The range for the Norway rat is wherever man has settled. An immigrant from Europe, it reached the New World at the beginning of the American Revolution. By the thousands this animal stowed away in covered wagons and trains heading west, establishing populations in villages and towns across the country. So prolific was their movement that in the early part of this century these rats outnumbered humans.

A person would be hard-pressed if he had to think of a benefit provided by these countless freeloaders. The Norway rat's lifestyle is one of destruction and sabotage. Almost any packaging is susceptible to the rat's gnawing, making such foods as vegetables, grains, meats, and fruit readily available. They have been known to chew through lead pipes for water and strip insulation from electrical wires resulting in short circuits and fires. Another negative aspect is their menace as disease carriers, which includes trichinosis, typhus, rabies, and bubonic plague. In this area, the Norway rat does not fare well in the wild. They are mostly restricted to buildings in cities, towns, and rural areas, or to the accompanying garbage dumps and sewage disposal systems.

Norway rat   J. CUNNINGHAM

House Mouse   *Mus musculus*

Another immigrant from Europe is the common house mouse. They discovered the easiest lifestyle was to move in with man. Occasionally their presence is discovered by actual sightings, but most often a hole in a cereal box or a chewed corner on a cellophane package gives them away.

Any pilfered soft material provides bedding for nests which can be located in woodpiles, walls, dresser drawers, or sofa furniture. The fact that they are able to mate at two months of age and produce five litters a year (each averaging eight offspring) should give you some idea of their ability to proliferate. With much effort, ninety-five percent of the mouse population could be destroyed, only to have the remaining few restore the numbers in no time. This mouse is distinguished from all others by a brown coat that turns to gray — never white — on the underbelly.

Deer Mouse   *Peromyscus maniculatus*

To best identify this mouse look for its white feet and its long, bicolored tail. Their ears are also rather large for a mouse and sparsely covered with short fine hairs. One's best chance to see this small rodent would be around vacation cabins in the mountains. As these structures are abandoned for the winter, *maniculatus* moves in immediately to set up housekeeping. It does not hibernate, so it builds a warm nest and actively seeks something to eat. This mouse does not cache food, and occasionally they starve to death during a long winter.

House mouse

Deer mouse

T. ULRICH

Bushy-tailed Woodrat

Neotoma cinerea

Although the name "rat" causes many people to take an immediate dislike to this animal, its life-style is clean and simple. The woodrat's residence is often marked by a pile of debris several feet high, consisting of sticks, manure, tin cans, litter, or anything easily carried: thus the nickname "pack rat."

The woodrat will often drop what he is carrying if a more appealing treasure catches his eye, which is why campers sometimes awaken to find strange items lying in place of their equipment.

"Trade rats " are mainly nocturnal, but will venture out during summer's longer days. Since they do not hibernate they must cache large amounts of food in their den. Many of the Park Service cabins along Lake McDonald in Glacier National Park have resident populations. Usually, the only real damage caused by this New World rat to humans is lost sleep due to their nocturnal habits.

Bushy-tailed woodrat   T. Ulrich

Woodrat nest   T. Ulrich

Bushy tail   T. Ulrich

Meadow Vole   *Microtus pennsylvanicus*

Preferring the understory of tall grass, the meadow vole goes about his business along groomed "runways." Various side branches lead to foraging areas, toilets, or escape openings to his lair. Active day or night, he tends to his network of paths leaving discarded stems neatly piled along the side.

His brief appearances, small size, and brown fur often cause him to be called "meadow mouse." An extended view would reveal a shortened tail, small ears, brownish long fur, and small bead-like eyes — all characteristics more closely attributed to a vole.

The life span for a meadow vole is just short of a year. If they have not succumbed to any of a long line of predators, their energetic lifestyle often leads to cardiac arrest. But during their short prolific life, they have the ability to start mating at two months of age. Combine this with a short twenty-one day gestation period and the ability to produce six to eight litters a year, and one can understand why meadow voles occasionally number over 100 individuals per acre.

The best way to find a meadow vole would be to locate their well-groomed runways. By parting the grass a little and remaining quiet and still, you should be able to see the little meadow mouse scampering by as it checks all its passageways.

Meadow vole 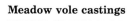   J. Wassink

Meadow vole castings   J. Wassink

Unidentified juvenile vole   J. Wassink

Muskrat

Ondatra zibethicus

This aquatic rat is named for its two prominent musk glands located at the base of its abdomen. The musk is highly concentrated to keep it from being dispersed in the watery habitat. It is used mainly during the breeding season to stake out territorial boundaries and attract the opposite sex.

Home for the muskrat can be a pond, marsh, reservoir, stream, irrigation ditch or wherever there is a constant non-fluctuating water level. The lodge is constructed of cattails, rushes, and other aquatic plants in a shallow body of water. This dwelling usually has two underwater entrances and a dry nesting area above the high water mark. When feeding, the muskrat carries aquatic plants to a favorite location away from the lodge. He eats the soft tender parts and lets the rest accumulate to form feeding platforms. Used regularly, these platforms are occasionally roofed over, creating a feeding lodge.

Muskrats that inhabit rivers or streams do not build houses but live in holes in the bank. Entrances are underwater, and the nest chamber is kept well above water's highest mark.

Muskrats do not hibernate and are active all year. A unique ability to close their lips behind the four incisor teeth allows this mammal to prune aquatic vegetation under the ice. Carried back to one of its lodges, the food is devoured in privacy.

Since they have the ability to produce two or more litters a year, it seems muskrats should be everywhere. This is not so, because they are an important food source for many animals from great horned owls to coyotes, with mink taking the greatest toll.

Muskrats consistently capitalize on the handiwork of the beaver, even to the point of inhabiting the same lodge. If you wish to view this shy creature while visiting the Northern Rockies, sit a while by a beaver lodge and you just might get a double treat.

Muskrat   T. Ulrich

Feeding platform   T. Ulrich

Muskrat lodge   T. Ulrich

Beaver

Castor canadensis

"Architect," "woodcutter," "builder," and oftentimes "nuisance" are words that characterize America's largest rodent, the beaver. Any running waterway is subject to his disapproval. He starts by anchoring small sticks in the streambed, then this eager bundle of energy utilizes the current to carry and push more material, eventually forming an interwoven heap. Water collects, leaks are chinked with mud, more sticks, and more mud, creating a much larger body of water: a beaver pond. Fish love it, the landscape drinks from it, ducks play in it, and spring rains collect there for the dry season — all positive aspects of the pond. But when irrigation ditches are blocked, roads are flooded, or someone's fruit trees are destroyed, the conflict always results in trapping and transplanting.

No other animal played a larger role in the early development of our nation than the beaver. Trappers scoured the west for beavers when a high price for its fur in Europe created a rush in this country second only to the gold rush. A lucky change in fashion saved this rodent from extinction and gave it a new lease on life.

Currently the pelts are not worth much, but something else has put a price on their head. Castoreum, a yellowish substance, is secreted by a large gland whose duct opens through the cloaca. Deposited along the water's edge, castoreum is used to scent-mark territory and attract the opposite sex. Thought to be a cure-all for every ailment known to man, untold numbers of beavers are massacred for the castor gland.

When establishing a new territory, the beaver follows a set order of events. First, a den is built, creating a pond that is deep enough not to freeze during winter. Next, a lodge is built for shelter, with an underwater entrance and dry sleeping chamber. Finally, a mass of sticks called a cache is collected near the lodge to provide nourishment during the long winter.

Beaver T. Ulrich

Swimming beaver T. Ulrich

Beaver pond T. Ulrich

The beaver does not hibernate and is active all winter. Under the ice, he feeds from the cache. As during other times of the year, he chews bark to get at the nutritious cambium layer. Fat stored in the tail is utilized during these lean times. A favorite tree and food source is quaking aspen. Leaves and aquatic vegetation are also listed high on the menu. Chewing on fibrous wood regularly wears the four prominent incisor teeth away. These teeth grow continuously so they must be worn down because too much growth would inhibit feeding.

To keep from freezing in the chilly water, much time is spent grooming and oiling the fur with the comb claw of the hind foot. Oil is produced from a gland at the base of the tail and works as an excellent water repellent. A layer of air trapped next to the skin is warmed and insulates effectively.

Beaver are very sociable, and a colony often includes eight to ten members comprised of two adults and two generations of offspring. As newborn arrive each year, the older generations leave to establish their own territory. This is a critical time, because they become vulnerable to predators while migrating to new areas. In its own pond, the beaver has few predators.

While visiting Glacier National Park, the oxbow on Lower McDonald Creek provides an excellent opportunity to view beaver. Just as the evening sun drops behind Apgar Mountain, you can often see them entering and leaving the lodge.

Bringing home a meal T. Ulrich

Beaver cache T. Ulrich

Beaver's lodge on the bank T. Ulrich

Northern Pocket Gopher   *Thomomys talpoides*

Noted for the large fur-lined shopping bags beside each cheek, the pocket gopher prefers soft soil where it can mine for bulbs and roots. Its tunnels are an aimless pattern of interconnecting passageways, clearly mapped by piles of discarded soil. As the burrows are dug, excavated dirt is deposited on the surface. The exit is left open until the job is finished, then tightly backfilled, shutting out all potential enemies.

With the aid of large front claws, the gopher digs for its favorite plant material. Excess amounts are packed into its pouches and carried to storage rooms. Along its maze of tunnels are found many rooms — one may be used as a den, one for storage, and also one as a bathroom.

This rodent does not hibernate, but available food can be dug for year round. During winter, tunnels are readily excavated in the snow. These are then packed with soil brought up from underground. As the snow melts, these earthen casts (about two inches wide) remain. Like earthworms, these gophers are invaluable for the amount of soil turned over and the underground ventilation they provide. There is little chance of ever seeing a pocket gopher, as their subterranean lifestyle seldom brings them to the surface. One is usually satisfied with seeing their handiwork on the surface of the ground.

Northern pocket gopher   A. Nelson

Gopher castings   T. Ulrich

Northern Flying Squirrel   *Glaucomys sabrinus*

Although this animal is clearly labeled as a flying squirrel, this is a misnomer, because they are totally incapable of ascending or sustaining height. Equipped with a large excess fold of skin from each wrist to ankle, a quick leap with appendages outstretched catches the air allowing them to glide to the safety of another tree.

To observe them gliding is a marvel of nature. With some quick head movements in a triangular motion, the squirrel checks distance and depth. Once the leap is made, its downward descent picks up speed quickly. On approach to their landing tree, momentum is slowed by inclining upward, resulting in a four-point landing aginst the trunk. Their flight is controlled by manuevering the flying membranes and using the flattened tail as a rudder.

It has been said that the flying squirrel is the most numerous squirrel in the forest. Yet, hardly any outdoor person ever sees one. The reason is that this squirrel spends all daylight hours sound asleep in the darkness of an old woodpecker hole. Awake all night, it caches acorns, pine nuts, and fungi, or it feeds on boreal lichens and mushrooms.

If you'd like to view this squirrel, a kick to a tree with a woodpecker hole will occasionally cause a sleepy-eyed squirrel to peek out. If you watch a bird feeder at night, you might also catch one pilfering these stores under cover of darkness.

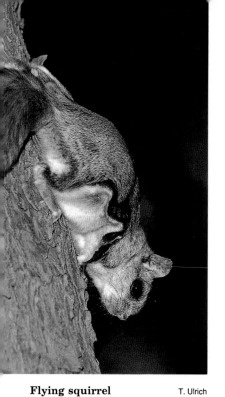

Flying squirrel   T. Ulrich

Flying squirrel   T. Ulrich

Flying squirrel   T. Ulrich

Sleepy-eyed   T. Ulrich

123

Red Squirrel   *Tamiasciurus hudsonicus*

Your first clue to the presence of this small tree squirrel will probably be a vocal scolding for intruding its territory. The loud chattering, which carries well through the woods, has given it another appropriate name: "Chickaree." This small bundle of energy is familiar with every branch in its domain and consequently every escape route.

The red squirrel's preferred den is an old woodpecker hole — especially in winter. During summer the cavity is often insect-infested, so the squirrel constructs a leaf nest in the upper reaches of a tree next to the trunk. Large amounts of cones, seeds, and fungi are cached for winter. A single vertical tunnel in the snow will make the entire cache available. When harvesting fungi, it is a customary procedure of the red squirrel to let the mushroom dry on a branch before storing. Remember also that a red squirrel can eat fungi poisonous to humans, therefore this is not a practical method of finding edible mushrooms.

In the Northern Rockies the red squirrel is common to all national parks and wilderness areas. The best thing to do is listen carefully; your ears will tell your eyes where to look.

Fox Squirrel   *Sciurus niger*

The fox squirrel is not very common in this area. It can occasionally be found along the river bottoms of the Missouri and Yellowstone; there are also some transplanted populations established in Missoula and Hamilton. One such population can be viewed on the campus of the University of Montana in Missoula.

Being a rather heavy-bodied squirrel, it cannot match the arboreal antics of smaller gray or red cousins. Being slower, the fox squirrel would also be easy prey for a predator like the pine marten. This squirrel has a preferred taste for acorns and this is also a limiting factor in this area.

The common name stretches your imagination, as it originates from the reddish-orange fur similar to a red fox. Interestingly, the scientific title *niger* means black. The first fox squirrel encountered by Linnaeus when he named the species was in the rare melanistic phase.

Red squirrel   8-14-2013   T. Ulrich

Cone cache   T. Ulrich

Fox squirrel   T. Ulrich

Black-tailed Prairie Dog   *Cynomys ludovicianus*

The presence of prairie dogs is easily detected by numerous earthen dikes scarring the landscape. These conical mounds occasionally rise two feet high, provide excellent lookout points, and keep flood waters from flushing out the burrows. The prairie dog is very gregarious. It is common to see hundreds of hillocks scattered across the open plains. The light of each day finds a myriad of these prairie rodents active in the vicinity of their mounds, collectively called a "town." Territorialism is important. Each town is further subdivided into smaller precincts or "neighborhoods." Prairie dogs can go freely in their own neighborhood, but cannot venture to the next as they will be driven away.

Since it is a member of the rodent family, one may wonder about its misleading name. The "dog" comes from their warning call which sounds like a bark. As members of the town feed or go about their business, one or several continually act as sentries. At the slightest sign of danger they give a warning bark. Their only protection is in the burrow where they usually sit a few feet from the entrance and listen for the slightest sound. These prairie dogs are only found along the eastern edge of the Northern Rockies.

White-tailed Prairie Dog   *Cynomys leucurus*

Listed as an endangered species, the white-tail's range just touches the southeastern edge of the Northern Rockies. There is little competition between these animals and their close cousins, the black-tail. The white-tail is limited to narrow valleys between mountain ranges. White-tailed dog towns tend to be small, comprising never more than two hundred individuals. They also lack the conical earthen mounds surrounding their burrow entrance. Usually colonizing a slope, all dirt is pushed on a pile directly in front of the burrow. One's chances of seeing this prairie dog are slim at best.

Black-tailed prairie dog

Barking

White-tailed prairie dog $8-11/2013$

Golden-mantled
Ground Squirrel   *Spermophilus lateralis*

Because of the broad white stripe down each side, this species is often mistaken for a chipmunk. The golden-mantled's chestnut cape, larger size, and lack of facial stripes make it distinctive, but it is still called "golden chipmunk" since both species are often seen together.

Although it is classified as a true ground squirrel, the golden-mantled will climb trees in search of seeds or fruit. They fill their cheeks and store the loot in their burrows, causing some speculation as to when this cache is utilized. Being a true hibernator, the squirrel either wakes during the winter to feed or uses it in spring when food might be in short supply.

Squirrels which have their burrow near an area of heavy human traffic become quite tame. Most people find their begging to be cute and consequently bombard the animal with an assortment of junk food. Remember, it is unlawful to feed any animal in any national park.

Thirteen-lined
Ground Squirrel   *Spermophilus tridecemlineatus*

Easily identified, this distinctive ground squirrel actually has thirteen alternating dark and light stripes extending the length of its body. Originally, its range stretched from the Rockies east to Indiana, where it was commonly called "striped gopher." The westward movement of farming forced this ground squirrel to feed on grain, consequently leading to its elimination in many areas.

This striped ground squirrel is not as colonial as many of its relatives. There is more distance between burrows, but protection in numbers remains an important factor. The entrance hole lacks the mound of bare soil commonly seen among other ground squirrels. It is customary to have two burrows: a shallow one for summer use and a deeper one for winter hibernation. A typical burrow consists of a short vertical shaft with many lateral side branches, several storage rooms, and a nesting chamber.

A stable population of these ground squirrels inhabits a small isolated area in the Belly River Valley of Glacier National Park.

Golden-mantled ground squirrel   8-13-2013   T. Ulrich

Golden-mantled ground squirrel   T. Ulrich

Thirteen-lined ground squirrel   T. Ulrich

Columbian
Ground Squirrel
Spermophilus columbianus

In Northwest Montana, the Columbian ground squirrel is an important protein food source for most of the predators. Birds of prey, weasels, canines, felines, and bears take a high percentage of these squirrels. The squirrel's reproductive efficiency ensures a never-ending supply. These squirrels often store small quantities of food for possible use in spring before lush new growth arrives. Their burrows are deep, extending well below the frost line. They are true hibernators, retiring in late September and awakening in June. During this time their body temperature drops to 37 degrees F, their pulse drops to five beats per minute, and one breath is taken every five minutes.

Glacier National Park is thoroughly populated with this ground squirrel — they are very easily seen around the Logan Pass Visitors Center.

Columbian ground squirrel   T. Ulrich

8-13-2019

Columbian ground squirrel   T. Ulrich

Uinta Ground Squirrel *Spermophilus armatus*

The Uinta is the most common ground squirrel found in Yellowstone Park. A good identifying characteristic is the black tail hairs which are lightly tipped. Because they prefer to dig their burrows in moist habitat, areas near the Madison River are heavily populated with *armatus*. This squirrel is also a long hibernator. Oftentimes adults will enter the den during summer cold snaps and estivate. Young from each year tend to stay out longer to build body fat for the long winter.

Richardson's
Ground Squirrel *Spermophilus richardsonii*

A very characteristic habit of flicking its tail while on all fours gave this ground squirrel a common name of "Flicker Tail." Before agriculture conquered the plains of Minnesota to the Rocky Mountains, Richardson's was more abundant than the prairie dog. Densites of fifty individuals per acre were common. When foraging, this squirrel fills its cheek pouches with seeds, then transfers these to storage chambers deep within the burrow. As crops were sown, the toll on farmers' seeds led to the extermination of most of the Richardson's population. They are true hibernators. A plain smoky-gray coat distinguishes it from all other ground squirrels.

Uinta ground squirrel   J. Lange

Richardson's ground squirrel   T. Ulrich

Hoary Marmot *Marmota caligata*

"Whistler" and "Whistle Pig" are common names for this ground hog of the alpine. In this vast openness, the hoary marmot reacts to the slightest possibility of danger by emitting a loud shrill repetitive whistle as it scurries to dive into the sanctuary of a burrow. Birds of prey, a passing grizzly, a wolverine, or a mountain lion might all prey upon this rodent, which can weigh up to twenty pounds. Its distinctive hoary (grayish-white) appearance makes it easy to identify, but interestingly, its scientific title *caligata* means "booted," referring to its conspicuous black feet.

Like all of its cousins — the yellow-bellied, Vancouver, and Olympic marmots and the woodchuck — this marmot is a true hibernator. With such a short active season, most of its time is spent feeding desperately to build body supplies. In late September, one finds all of them closed in their sleeping chamber well below the frostline. The marmot's body temperature drops to 36 degrees F, respiration slows to one breath every five minutes, and heart rate is only five beats per minute. Hoary remains in this state during the long cold winter, then emerges in spring, occasionally by tunneling up through ten feet of snow.

Any of the trails from Logan Pass in Glacier National Park pass through excellent hoary marmot habitat. The prime time to view and photograph this diurnal creature is just as the sun comes over the horizon. After spending the night in a cold damp burrow, they are eager to sunbathe on a nice warm rock.

Hoary marmot   T. Ulrich

Friendly greeting   T. Ulrich

Young marmot   T. Ulrich

Yellow-bellied Marmot   *Marmota flaviventris*

Its name comes not from being a coward; instead (as you might suspect) it is derived from the color of its underbelly. The rich golden-yellow fur is most obvious when this marmot stands tall on an observation point. In close vicinity it utilizes clefts of rocks, spaces beneath boulders, or coarse rocky soil as a den site. This increases the difficulty any predator might have in trying to dig them out. Their several den openings are all avenues of escape usually interconnected by well-worn trails.

There are also characteristic "runways" which led to favorite feeding areas within the limits of their territories. Continually alert, any sign of danger causes them to give a loud whistle as they scamper to the safety of a burrow. These marmots are very colonial. The interconnecting tunnels are a maze few predators can follow or dig out.

Activity is strictly diurnal. The first rays of morning sunshine will find these marmots venturing about. One habitual practice at this time is to perch on a nearby rock allowing the sun to rid them of the chill of underground nights. Like all marmots they are true hibernators. Whereas Glacier Park is noted for hoary marmots, Yellowstone Park lays claim as the yellow-belly capitol. The location of the marmot colonies is common knowledge in the park; just ask any park ranger for directions.

Yellow-bellied marmot

Yellow-bellied marmot

Yellow-pine Chipmunk
Tamias amoenus

The best identifying characteristic for a yellow-pine is its distinctive bicolored ears. Other than that, the yellow-pine and the red-tailed chipmunk are so similar, some mammalogists feel both species are the same.

These inquisitive little animals have a preference for areas with fallen trees. The downed trunks provide excellent highways to foraging areas or numerous hiding places when the yellow-pine is being pursued by predators. Dens tend to be underground, terminating at a nest chamber. It is believed that chipmunks are partial hibernators — they awaken periodically to feed on cached stores.

Red-tailed Chipmunk
Tamias ruficaudus

Take a good look to verify the red or rufus tail, especially on the ventral side — this is the best characteristic for identifying this chipmunk. Spending much of its time on the ground, the red-tailed chipmunk will occasionally climb trees for seeds. During times of plenty, excess food is cached deep in their winter dens. One interesting event caught my attention as a chipmunk was repeatedly filling its cheeks from a bird feeder. After each trip from the food source, it went to a number of trees in the same general direction. I later examined those same trees and found clumps of bird seed stuck to the bark with the aid of saliva. I imagined his den was already full from other pilferings of the feeder.

In Glacier Park, a short hike to Avalanche Lake provides two excellent opportunities to view nature. You can experience a beautiful cirque lake of emerald waters and at the same time view the numerous red-tailed chipmunks which scamper about the area.

Yellow-pine chipmunk   8-15-2013   T. Ulrich

Gathering straw   T. Ulrich

Red-tailed chipmunk   T. Ulrich

Desert Cottontail

Sylvilagus audubonii

The range of this cottontail just reaches the southeastern edge of the Northern Rockies. Its home is the open, arid sagebrush areas common throughout Wyoming. Here, finding shelter of thick brush, it spends much of its time sitting in a form of dried vegetation.

Compared to a mountain cottontail, *audubonii* is somewhat paler. To distinguish between the two, look carefully at the ears. The desert cottontail has noticeably longer ears and the tips tend to be darker. Even an untrained eye should have little trouble identifying these two rabbits by their ears.

Young are born naked and have closed eyes like all true rabbits. A fur-lined nest contains two to five offspring which are nursed usually only once a day. The line of predators is a long one and less exposure is beneficial for both her and the young. These cottontails are unimportant except for their aesthetic value and their role as a food source for other wildlife.

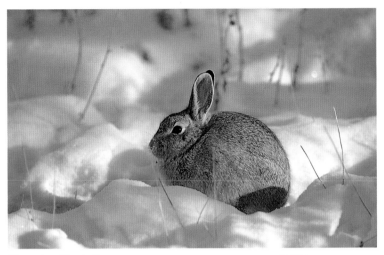

Desert cottontail   T. Ulrich

Desert cottontail   T. Ulrich

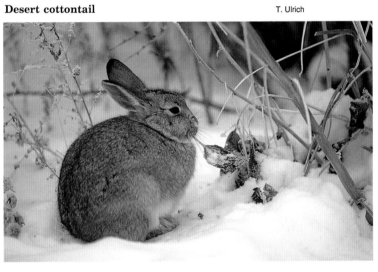

Nuttall's (Mountain) Cottontail
Sylvilagus nuttallii

Nuttall's cottontail is the most common rabbit found in the Northern Rockies. Although the jackrabbit is also a resident of this area, it is really a hare. The main difference between the two lies with the newborn. Cottontails are born hairless with eyes shut while hares are fully furred and have their eyes open.

The mortality rate among cottontails is one of the highest for any mammal. A long line of predators — including birds of prey, coyote, fox, bobcat, and weasel — all dine readily upon this lagomorph. Their toll is so heavy that eighty-five percent of all offspring never reach their first birthday. The only defenses cottontails have are their speed, jumping ability, and incredible reproduction rate. Four to five litters a year each averaging five young are possible even with the shortened season of the Northern Rockies.

This mountain rabbit's gestation period is short at twenty-eight days. Just prior to giving birth, the expectant mother will dig a bowl-shaped depression in the ground. Fur will then be pulled from the belly area exposing the nipples. This fur is mixed with vegetation making a bed and cover for the nest. The helpless young are nursed on a rich, butterfat milk. During this time the offspring are susceptible to a wide range of environmental influences as rains drown, late snows freeze, or hot sun bakes them. Almost immediately after giving birth, the female will venture off to be mated again, thus producing the numbers to withstand a high first year mortality.

This rabbit is most active at daybreak and again as the sun sets below the horizon. The rest of its uneventful life is spent seeking refuge under a brush pile or in the deep recess of a rocky slope. Occasionally this rabbit will make a traditional "form" from long vegetation, but it generally prefers a more protected domain.

Mountain cottontail J. Wassink

Cottontail nest T. Ulrich

143

White-tailed Jackrabbit   *Lepus townsendii*

The common name "jackrabbit" is a misnomer as its newborn more closely fit the definition of a hare — born with eyes open and fully furred. Nursed briefly after their birth, the young cut their teeth very quickly and are soon on their own, sampling all vegetation.

The white-tailed jackrabbit is the largest of all lagomorphs, often standing eighteen inches tall and weighing six pounds. Their great height is aided by extremely long ears, always black-tipped. Very sensitive to any sound, the ears also serve a secondary purpose — lined with minute blood capillaries, they help in dispersing body heat.

Each period of darkness is an extensive feeding time. After consuming nearly a pound of vegetation, this jackrabbit is usually back in its form by the first break of daylight. Each jack has three or four personal forms scattered about its territory. These resting places are generally under cover of a bush. Here, protected from the sun and not easily seen, the jack sits and sleeps. Movement of his feet in this small cramped area creates a shallow bowl devoid of vegetation.

The jackrabbit prefers to sit undetected if an intruder passes near, but at any moment the jackrabbit could bolt from its form and quickly speed away. When pursued, the jack can outrun any predator; speeds of forty-five miles per hour are easily attained. While on the run, periodic observation jumps are made to check progress of the pursuer.

In the more northern part of this hare's range, there is a pronounced change of color to a winter white. During summer and at lower latitudes, the tawny brown coat is kept all year. An excellent place to view this animal is at the Gardiner Flats on the edge of Yellowstone Park. Take a leisurely walk into the lower foothills and you will surely scare up this huge jackrabbit.

White-tailed jackrabbit   T. ULRICH

Built for speed   T. ULRICH

Winter pelage   T. ULRICH

Snowshoe Hare   *Lepus americanus*

The ability to change from a brown summer coat to a white winter coat and equip themselves with large furry feet makes this hare one of the more elusive prey. When the first snows are due, a complete molt takes place. Brown hairs are replaced by white ones, ensuring the hare's protective coloration. The large snowshoe feet not only allow escape from most predators (who get bogged down in the snow), but each new snowfall lifts the hare closer to brush which was out of reach during summer.

Where ranges overlap, one predator, the Canadian lynx, can match snow maneuverability with the hare. This cat also grows large snowshoe feet, allowing it to match the hare stride for stride over the surface of the snow.

The relationship between hare and lynx is a close one. This bond is easily understood when the hare's population cycle is examined. Peak numbers occur about every ten years, and the lynx population peaks one year later. What determines these cycles is still unknown.

Much of the life of this lagomorph is spent sitting in one of its many "forms." These forms are not well constructed, compared to those of the cottontail; the hare relies more on its coloration for concealment. The Northern Rockies are well-endowed with snowshoes. During early morning, one can find them feeding along the road in our national parks. A short hike in the woods might also scare one from its form.

Summer snowshoe hare 8-16-2013   T. Ulrich

Eclipse pelage   T. Ulrich

Winter pelage   T. Ulrich

Pika

Ochotona princeps

This little critter of the talus slopes is usually heard before it is seen. When alarmed, the pika sounds a characteristic "eek! eek!" to warn off intruders, but this sound can also be used to announce territorial claims. The pica's home of interconnecting tunnels is created by rocks or boulders at least 1.5 feet in diameter. This maze of natural passageways often discourages a weasel trying to trail the scurrying pika.

Due to two extra incisor teeth in the upper jaw, the pika is related to a rabbit. The pika is the size of a guinea pig. Its short rounded ears, small feet, cleft lip, and total lack of a tail have given it such common names as "rockrabbit," "cony," and "Little Chief Hare."

The pika has the unique habit of cutting vegetation and piling it in haystacks to dry in the sun. After curing, this dry salad is stored in protected hollows to be used during winter, a time when this critter is active deep under snow. As many as twenty different species of plants can be found in any one haystack, showing the diversity of vegetation consumed.

Comparatively little is known about the life history of the pika. The scant information recorded is from observations as they scamper about the rocky surface, but what happens deep in its labyrinth can only be speculated. Glacier and Yellowstone national parks have prolific populations of pika. If you wish to observe these little rock lagomorphs, keep your ears open, they will tell your eyes where to look.

Pika   T. Ulrich

Collecting for a haystack   T. Ulrich

Haystack   T. Ulrich

Little Brown Bat
Myotis lucifugus

The little brown bat is commonly seen during summer, usually near water. The head and body are only two inches long, and it weighs only a quarter of an ounce. Olive-brown in color, its wings and tail membrane are nearly black and almost totally free of hair. It is very gregarious, although a roost may be comprised of just a few individuals. Each evening as the sun sets, this bat leaves the colony in its quest for insects which are always caught while the bat is in flight. Due to its poor eyesight, all prey and surroundings are located by sonar detection. A high pitched, oral sound is made. The resulting echo off every object in the vicinity is received and interpreted for location, distance, shape, etc. It would seem that each time a sound is emitted, the new sound would mix with the echo, but to control this, a small flap of skin called a "tragus" seals off the ear opening when the bat sends out a new signal.

Townsend's Big-eared Bat
Plecotus townsendii

This bat is easily identified by its extremely large ears. These enormous detectors of sound are nearly 1.5 inches long. Also look for a lump which will be present on each side of the muzzle just in front of the eyes. The members of this species live individually or in small colonies. There is a good possibility this bat will hibernate all winter in caves or in structures having cave conditions.

Little brown bat

J. Wassink

Townsend's big-eared bat

K. Dubois

Vagrant Shrew   *Sorex vagrans*

Shrews are the smallest American mammal. Their total body length seldom reaches five inches, of which close to half will be tail. They are insectivorous by nature, but we know relatively little about their lifestyle. One general characteristic of shrews is their need for a continual food supply. Their small size lets so much body heat escape that they must eat often to replace this loss. It is estimated that some shrews consume an amount of food equal to their own weight every three hours. They forage for food and perform daily activities in almost total darkness since their eyes are tiny and poorly developed. Long whiskers are used to help follow the maze of runways used constantly.

Vagrans is Latin and means "wandering." Your only chance of seeing this shrew would be while it hurriedly uses its runways. Its head narrows to a long, pointed nose and color is reddish-brown above turning to a gray shade below.

Vagrant shrew   J. Wassink

Portrait   J. Wassink

153

Glossary

Albinistic: whitish, having less than the normal amount of pigment.

Canid: of or like a dog.

Canine tooth: tooth between the incisors and the premolars, eyetooth.

Carnivorous: flesh eating animal.

Cloaca: a common cavity into which the intestine, and occasionally the urinary and generative canals open.

Digitigrade: walk primarily on the toes.

Diurnal: day loving.

Estivation: a temporary state of torpor.

Estrus: state of sexual excitability during which the female of most mammals will accept the male.

Fauna: the animals of a given region.

Form: protected, hidden abode of vegetation where a lagomorph passes time.

Gestation period: period of carrying the young, from conception to birth.

Gregarious: spending much time in numbers.

Guard hairs: long pigmented hairs for protection.

Habitat: natural area where an animal lives.

Harem: group of females serviced by one male.

Herbivore: plant-eating animal.

Incisor: front teeth between canines.

Indigenous: originating in the region where found.

Lagomorph: belonging to the rabbit family.

Melanistic: blackish, having abnormal amount of dark pigment.

Nocturnal: active in the night.

Omnivorous: flesh and plant eating animal.

Pelage: hair on a mammal.

Plantigrade: walk on entire foot from heel to toe.

Polygamous: having more than one mate at the same time.

Precocial: well developed at birth and able to run about.

Predator: animals which live by preying upon other animals.

Prolific: to produce offspring abundantly.

Retractile: capable of being withdrawn.

Species: a group of animals or plants exhibiting certain permanent characteristics in common.

Tine: branch of an antler off the main beam.

Tragus: flap of skin near the bottom of the external ear opening in bats.

Underfur: soft hair hidden by the coarse guard hairs, aids in warmth.

Ungulate: walks on toenails or hooves.

Velvet: soft membrane of blood vessels which secrete calcium to the inside, depositing the boney antler.

Index

We encourage you to patronize your local bookstore. Most stores will order any title they do not stock. You may also order directly from Mountain Press, using the order form provided below or by calling our toll-free, 24-hour number and using your VISA, MasterCard, Discover or American Express.

Some other Natural History titles of interest:

____Amphibians and Reptiles of Montana	$20.00
____Awesome Ospreys: Fishing Birds of the World	$12.00
____Birds of the Northern Rockies	$12.00
____Birds of the Pacific Northwest Mountains	$14.00
____Edible and Medicinal Plants of the West	$21.00
____An Introduction to Northern California Birds	$14.00
____An Introduction to Southern California Birds	$14.00
____An Introduction to Southern California Butterflies	$22.00
____Loons: Diving Birds of the North	$12.00
____Nature's Yucky! Gross Stuff That Helps Nature Work	$10.00
____Nature's Yucky! 2: The Desert Southwest	$12.00
____Northwest Weeds	$14.00
____Organic Gardening in Cold Climates	$12.00
____Owls: Whoo are they?	$12.00
____Raptors of the Rockies	$16.00
____Sagebrush Country: A Wildflower Sanctuary	$14.00
____Watchable Birds of the Black Hills, Badlands, and Northern Great Plains	$22.00
____Watchable Birds of the Great Basin	$16.00
____Watchable Birds of the Southwest	$14.00
____Wild Berries of the West	$16.00
____Wildflowers of Montana	$22.00
____Wyoming Wildflowers	$19.00

Shipping and handling: 1 to 4 books, add $3.50; 5 or more books, add $5.00

Send the books marked above. I enclose $_____

Name_____

Address_____

City_____State_____Zip_____

☐ Payment enclosed (check or money order in U.S. funds)

Bill my: ☐VISA ☐MasterCard ☐Discover ☐American Express

Card No._____Exp. Date:_____

Security Code:_____Signature _____

MOUNTAIN PRESS PUBLISHING COMPANY
P.O. Box 2399 • Missoula, MT 59806
Order Toll Free 1-800-234-5308 • Have your credit card ready.
e-mail: info@mtnpress.com • website: www.mountain-press.com